W9-BOO-471

blue jean buddha
voices of young buddhists

blue jean BUDDHA

VOICES Of YOUNG BUDDHISTS

EDITED BY SUMI LOUNDON

FOREWORD BY JACK KORNFIELD

WISDOM PUBLICATIONS • BOSTON

PALATINE PUBLIC LIBRARY DISTRICT
700 N. NORTH COURT
PALATINE, ILLINOIS 60067-8159

Wisdom Publications
199 Elm Street
Somerville MA 02144 USA
www.wisdompubs.org

© 2001 Sumi D. Loundon

All rights reserved.

No part of this book may be reproduced in any form or by
any means, electronic or mechanical, including photogra-
phy, recording, or by any information storage and retrieval
system or technologies now known or later developed,
without the permission in writing from the publisher.

Library of Congress Cataloging-in-Publication Data
Blue jean Buddha : voices of young Buddhists / edited by
Sumi Loundon ; foreword by Jack Kornfield.
       p. cm.
    ISBN 0-86171-177-7 (alk. paper)
    1. Youth, Buddhist—United States—Biography. 2. Spiritual
biography—United States. 3. Youth, Buddhist—Religious life—
United States. I. Loundon, Sumi D., 1975–.
BQ738.B58 2001
294.3'0973'09051—dc21   2001033236

ISBN 0-86171-177-7

06 05 04 03 02
6   5   4   3   2

Cover design by Laura Shaw Feit
Interior by Gopa and Ted2

Wisdom Publications' books are printed on acid-free paper
and meet the guidelines for the permanence and durability
set by the Council on Library Resources.

Printed in the United States of America.

Dedicated to the dharma friends
who've helped me on the path
and to my parents.

May the merit from this book
be extended to the well-being of all.

TABLE OF CONTENTS

FOREWORD

WHAT IF BUDDHA WERE BORN in North America, in our times? From the comfort of his modern home might he begin to wander the streets of our world and see the same human conditions of aging, sickness, and death, the same human-created sufferings of greed, war, racism, and injustice that he saw in India 2,500 years ago? When he reached his twenties would he, again out of compassion, go forth from the palaces of comfort to seek liberation for the sake of all beings?

He has. His search for freedom and universal loving-kindness can be found in the voices and spirit of the young writers in this book—in their honesty, their courage, and their care. Though we live in a world troubled by ecological destruction, consumerism, and conflict, all who listen to their hearts can sense the possibility of humans—of each one of us— being more aware, more compassionate, more free. To sense this is to connect with our awakened heart, our buddha nature. The world needs this awakening more than ever, and a new generation has begun to draw on the Buddha's teaching to reawaken their noble hearts.

These young people's stories tell of finding the way of the Buddha here and now, in their very lives, in Buddhist communities and in practice in the world. Whether working in the prisons or climbing mountains, on the streets of New York or the sports field, their practice is honorable. From family struggles to social activism, from failure and success to reawak-ened passion for the world, these tales are full of dharma learning.

In Thailand, where I lived for some years as a monk, traditionally almost all young men and women would have to spend some time in their twenties undertaking spiritual practice in a monastery. Otherwise, the Elders would say their hearts would not become "ripe," that they would stay green like an unripened fruit. What is beautiful in this book is to see how the fruit of these contributors has begun to ripen.

As they ripen, wisdom replaces naïve excitement, judgment turns to compassion, and kindness deepens for self, for family, for all beings. This is the journey we all must take.

Finally, this new dharma generation asks important questions for the Buddhists of the twenty-first century. How do we balance meditation and social responsibility, dharma and mass media, monasticism and lay life? Do we take the Orient Express, or is there a new meeting of East and West that is our generation's way? It is these young Buddhists who will decide.

On the day I first ordained as a Buddhist monk in the forest monastery of the Elders, I had a strange experience. It felt oddly familiar, as if I had done it many times before. Of course, we can't say how these Blue Jean Buddhists have come to their wisdom, but maybe they are old Zen students, lamas, monks, and nuns reborn in the West. Whatever the source, what they have to teach us is inspiring. Now the dharma that is good in the beginning, good in the middle, and good in the end is in their good hearts and good hands.

Blessings,
Jack Kornfield
Spirit Rock Meditation Center
Woodacre, California
2001

A FEW YEARS AGO, I was working in the kitchen of a Buddhist retreat center settled in the woods of New England. The bright colors of autumn leaves were beginning to speckle the hillsides. I had just graduated from Williams College, where I had been cloistered in a world of perpetual youth. Now twenty-two, I suddenly found myself surrounded almost exclusively by copies of my parents, graying-haired Baby Boomers in their late forties and fifties. Working in the kitchen was a great way to meet these older Buddhists, who came in to scrub carrots, scrape plates, and dry pots. Our onion chopping was often slowed by conversations that started, "When I was your age…" followed by stories of how they got turned on to the dharma twenty or thirty years ago. I loved hearing their adventures about the time that was almost mythical in my mind, the '60s. Over the months, I became increasingly aware that we weren't just different in age and historical recollection. We were different in our maturity in the dharma and how we were relating Buddhism to our lives. They were thinking about integrating dharma into dealing with a teenage son, a midcareer change, divorce, picking socially responsible stocks, and retirement. I was questioning what Buddhism meant to me as someone just out of college, with no money and even less life-experience, still figuring out how to relate to my parents and my first real boyfriend, and just trying to get a basic understanding of who I was and wanted to be. Without peers to share my twenty-something stories and discuss issues, I began to feel somewhat lonely and isolated.

Where, I wondered, are the young Buddhists of today who should be inheriting the dharma from the older Buddhists? Are they like me, do they share the same questions and interests? If they exist, what kind of sangha are they creating? What does it mean to be a Buddhist in America today and where will we take it tomorrow? What challenges do we face? Given how few young Buddhists I knew, I became a little concerned that there would not be anyone to inherit the dharma. Who would be *my* dharma teacher when I was fifty? Who would run the centers and temples? As I finished a year of garlic peeling, lemon squeezing, and tossing burned experimental soups made from leftovers, I longed to discover the new generation of young Buddhists who were emerging in the West.

I began searching for young Buddhists by talking to the Buddhist parents and dharma teachers from the retreat center. Many of them had kids who had grown up with the dharma, though not all chose to keep it as part of their lives. From these young adults and their friends, through the internet and telephone, I branched out to hundreds of others across the country. Accumulating pages of notes about these young Buddhists from interviews, late-night conversations, and email exchanges, I started to see that we had certain questions in common: Should I consider life as a monastic, am I really a Buddhist, do I need a teacher, can I practice things from several traditions, should I try to learn an Asian language or go to Asia, can I just do meditation, what do my parents and friends think? I found myself learning a tremendous amount just by knowing there were others who had the same questions. Given these similar concerns, I began thinking that a book might be of interest, not just to older people wondering what the next breath of Buddhism will be, but also to young people who would like to meet their peers.

I envisioned a book that was some kind of literary sangha—a set of contributors—to serve as the basis for stimulating the larger sangha of both generations. I asked some of the amazing young people I had met over my three-year search to write about how they've brought the richness of the Buddhist tradition to bear on their lives. Within a few months, I found little gems piling into my email inbox that were direct, unpretentious, and moving. From the lessons of self-transformation to the variety of life stories to carrying dharma into livelihood, it is my hope that these narratives will inform and affirm the young Buddhist experience in America. In reading them, I found my own feeling for dharma deepening and my understanding of the contemporary Buddhist experience broadening.

From my learning and growth through compiling *Blue Jean Buddha* springs the Reflections section of this book. Here, I explore some of the questions and issues stemming from the contributors' essays that I feel are important for young Buddhists to be aware of and begin discussing. I center many of the questions around the social dimension because it is in the context of American society and modernization that I feel young Buddhists face a number of challenges that are critical to personal and communal development. I am reluctant to offer any answers, as almost all the questions are complex and remain unresolved not just for myself but for knowledgeable, long-time Buddhists as well.

Blue Jean Buddha does not reflect every variety of young Buddhist. I have sought to be inclusive in the range of ethnicities and lineages of traditional and newer Buddhisms, as well as to balance male and female. I tried to be sensitive to the fact that America is home not just to citizens but also to permanent residents and aliens who, for however long they are here, leave a lasting mark on Buddhism in America. I had hoped to be more inclusive in age range, touching especially on the teen years, but I found that teens tended to be early in their self-identification. Primarily, this book is composed of essays from people in their twenties, with a few from people who are in their early thirties. Most of the contributors are college-educated and would self-identify as Buddhist.

To fill in some of the gaps left open by this collection, I envision a companion volume that would include, for example, stories of those who practice in prison, teenagers, the queer community, those who wouldn't label themselves Buddhist but who do Buddhist things, those who've blended traditions, such as Jew-Bu's or UU-Bu's (that is, Jews and Unitarian Universalists practicing Buddhism), stories from young adults who've left Buddhism, those who live in the thriving ethnic Buddhist communities of America, married young couples raising children, inner-city practitioners, and so on. And yet, *Blue Jean Buddha* surveys a diverse group.

Through this presentation of an astonishing range of experiences, I hope that *Blue Jean Buddha* becomes as much a spiritual support and reference for others exploring Buddhism as the editing of this book has been for me.

Sumi Loundon
Cambridge, Massachusetts
May 2001

Acknowledgments

MANY KIND FRIENDS have given their skilled attention and aid to this book over the past three years. I am foremost deeply grateful to E. Gene Smith and Tim McNeill at Wisdom Publications for having faith that a book about young Buddhists was a publishable idea. Gene also read many versions of essays in the infant stages and provided excellent guidance spiced with humor. Josh Bartok, my editor at Wisdom Publications, himself a young Buddhist, has given intelligent and gentle editorial advice in the later stages of the manuscript. David Kittlestrom and Samantha Kent of Wisdom Publications also lent editorial support midway through the project.

A deep bow of appreciation goes to Dean Christopher Queen, my advisor at Harvard University, who enthusiastically took on my proposal. Chris's insightful comments were instrumental to discovering the overall structure and tone of the book from an initial jumble of ideas and scattered writings. His course on Buddhism in America was indispensable to my understanding of how young Buddhists are placed in this complex religious landscape.

Additionally on the academic end, I received excellent guidance from Dr. Andrew Olendzki and Mu Soeng at the Barre Center for Buddhist Studies. Five professors have also been indirectly related to the book but profoundly influential on my thinking about Buddhism in general, forcing me to question assumptions, namely, Professors George Dreyfus, Robert Gimello, Donald Swearer, Kenneth Kraft, and Charles Hallisey.

Numerous friends generously took time to read over manuscript parts to give me honest feedback. Khurram Hussain, the business manager at Wisdom, primarily entertained these wobbly first writings. Critical help on the manuscript was also given by Isa Loundon (my younger sister), Sabine Loundon (my grandmother), Tom and Amber Chand-Plunkett, Joshua Schrei, Amy Darling, Soren Gordhamer, Tom Patton, Marvin Belzer, David Zuniga, Natasha Judson, Il-mee Sunim, Josh Krieger, Paul Morris, and Seth Castleman. Of inspirational aid have been Matthew Daniell, Venerable Kunga Yeshe, Jonathan Stolzenberg, and Shari Epstein.

Several friends provided beautiful, quiet locations for me to do the actual writing and editing, for which I am grateful. I enjoyed the peaceful home of Gyano Gibson in rural Massachusetts, the aesthetic and vibrant home of Olivia and Harrison (Hob) Hoblitzelle in Cambridge, and Elijah and Emmanuelle Ary's groovy digs.

A number of institutions have been integral: many thanks to *Tricycle: The Buddhist Review* for hosting the original column that stimulated the whole idea of a book; to the staff and dharma teachers at Insight Meditation Society for the many wise dharma Baby Boomers who stayed up late in the night for armchair discussions and moral support; to the Barre Center for Buddhist Studies for providing an outstanding Buddhist library and idyllic spot for reflection; to the Harvard Buddhist Community, scholar-dharma friends who provided initial stories from which to expand.

I can hardly say enough good things about the kind and generous contributors to this volume, who opened their lives to me and provided the foundational narratives that comprise most of the book. They have patiently sustained many a developmental flogging from a young, inexperienced editor (me). Even those I've never met face-to-face feel like true brothers and sisters in the dharma.

Those Buddhist Biggies who provided stamps of approval I am indebted to: Sharon Salzberg was the first to enthusiastically offer her endorsement, followed by Daniel Goleman, Lama Surya Das, Professor Taitetsu Unno, China Galland, Daisaku Ikeda, Richard Seager, and

Zoketsu Norman Fischer. Most especially, my deep gratitude is for Jack Kornfield, who agreed over a hilarious cell-phone call on a Sunday evening to write the foreword.

Finally, my unbounded appreciation is for *mon compagne*, who provided unfailing enthusiasm, confidence when I became doubtful, and indispensable advice. He has been a wealth of wisdom and reflection about Buddhism, both ancient and contemporary. I could not have sustained the project without his unflagging support.

As it is with any large project, it can only be completed through the love and devotion of many hearts and minds. This book would not have been even remotely possible without the efforts and generosity of all these people. I bow in gratitude to each of you.

part one
LESSONS

INTRODUCTION

"I did a lot of drugs before I was Buddhist."
"Well, I did a lot of drugs *because* I was Buddhist."

"Was asking my girlfriend to get an abortion un-Buddhist?"

"I had a vision of the goddess Tara.
Was she real or was it just me projecting something?"

THESE WERE THE QUESTIONS that a few Buddhist friends and I discussed in a series of evening gatherings aimed at bringing dharma into our daily lives. Though many of our debates remained unresolved, we felt affirmed that creating a life around the Buddha's profound teachings gives rise to some critical and complex issues. What is the balance of medication and meditation for treating depression? Is the academic study of Buddhism an intellectual distraction or a complement to practice? Should one search for a Buddhist partner? Is the impetus to become a celibate monastic stemming from fear of intimate relationships or is it from a true desire for liberation? How should we interpret the five precepts: Is alcohol completely forbidden or is mindful drinking acceptable if one doesn't lose control? How can Buddhism be integrated into athletics, art, city life, and other religions? This section explores some of the questions that young Buddhists ask as their path in the dharma unfolds.

THE PERFECT BUDDHIST BOYFRIEND

Lillian Guild

"**A**SSHOLE!"
I screamed it with the full force of my being, slamming the door behind him as he walked silently out of my study. "Oh, God, did I really just say that?" I thought. The walls seemed to reverberate with the word, pushing me into a little ball. I curled up and began sobbing. How had I gone from being so in love with this man to screaming at him? I hated who I was becoming in this relationship, and I resented him for it. Memories flooded back of standing in front of my father as a little girl, of me feeling worthless, paralyzed, unable to defend myself as he screamed *Asshole!* and *Bitch!* at me for some little thing or another. I began crying so deeply that my throat locked in pain.

Where was my dignity? What a disaster this relationship was. This wasn't how I imagined it, having a Buddhist boyfriend; this wasn't how it was supposed to be.

———

When I was in college, there was a debate in the religious community about whether one needed to date someone of the same faith in order to have a deep, meaningful relationship. At the time, I dismissed the whole idea. After all, wasn't love supposed to transcend identity? My boyfriend was an atheist, and I saw him as more compassionate than some of my

LILLIAN GUILD, 31, IS WRITING UNDER A DIFFERENT NAME.

Christian friends who just talked about ethics all the time. But I often felt shy and self-conscious around him when it came to my Buddhist practice. At an early point in the relationship, I tested him by doing some morning prayers in Tibetan, lighting incense and candles, and quietly meditating while he sat in my worn recliner watching. As I was going down for a bow, I caught his smirk out of the corner of my eye. He tried to hide his amusement and disregard for my morning ritual, but it was too late. From that morning on, I rarely prayed in front of him. He was still in college when I graduated, and though we made promises to stay together, it quickly dissolved when I met Jasper, a muscular and handsome Buddhist who worked at the same nonprofit organization in Santa Fe as me.

wasn't love supposed to transcend identity?

Jasper became my first Buddhist boyfriend, and wow, did sparks fly! We meditated and chanted together, did yoga, and talked long into the night about dharma. It was like breathing pure oxygen. I felt myself growing as a practitioner. I felt supported and encouraged by him. I even felt our sex life was better because we liked to experiment with yogic energy circulation. We also brought a mindfulness to our relationship that made our time together very deep, very bonding. I began to ally myself with the other side of the religious-partner debate, believing that it was indeed essential to have a partner of the same faith.

About a year into the relationship, an older friend of mine, Donna, surprised me by commenting on how wonderful it must be to have a Buddhist relationship. Given how bad the relationship with her boyfriend was I could see why she'd think someone Buddhist might be better, but I still wondered why. Oh, she mused, you're so calm and peaceful from all the meditation, you try to be wise and compassionate, you don't focus heavily on yourself because you don't think the self exists, you have control of your emotions.

So that's how Jasper and I looked on the outside? But just because we aspire to understand no-self, to meditate, to be compassionate, doesn't mean that we were or we do. If we were all those things, we'd be buddhas already! But Donna's reasoning made some sense: having both been dharma bums for so many years, Jasper and I knew how to *appear* Buddhist. The right clothes were from dharma closets (free clothes left by wealthier retreatants), so they were just slightly shabby but not slouchy. The right hair was long and looked inexpensive. The right expression was serene or friendly. The right voice was soft and pleasing. The right speech never included anything negative, even if it needed to be expressed. The right sitting was on the cushion (definitely not a chair!), and retreats were mandatory. The right learning was to read the latest books, have a subscription to *Shambhala Sun* and *Tricycle*. The right worship was to have a nice altar, mumble prayers, and have some *mala* around the neck or wrist. *And*, the right partner was a meditating Buddhist. The problem was, I think we began to believe that these outward modes actually expressed some inner truth. In reality, many wounds festered. Our frustrations got hotter and hotter until that day, just a few months before we broke up, I screamed what previously had been unscreamable: "Asshole!"

I told Donna not to fool herself. Our relationship was just as violent, perhaps more so, than others I had seen. There was never any physical abuse, but we were constantly violating the respect and love we supposedly had for each other. Ironically, one of the biggest fights we had had to do with meditation practice. Jasper practiced a form of meditation that centered on cultivating compassion every morning and sometimes into the late evening. I'm not much of a meditator myself, but I did try to practice mindfulness of body, speech, and mind in everything I did. He needled me for not being able to sit on the cushion. I made fun of him for not bringing practice into his everyday life, for spending so many hours meditating. I preferred to wake up, check email, have a cup of tea, and listen to the latest news on NPR. He liked to wake up, do an hour

Just because we aspire to understand no-self doesn't mean we do.

of yoga, and then another hour or two of meditation. Because of our differences, we decided to keep separate rooms, which worked well until that one morning.

I had forgotten to get a notebook from his room the night before. He was doing the compassion meditation on a cushion as I entered the room as quietly as I could. Just as I was leaving, he exploded.

"Why are you disturbing my meditation when I've asked you so many times not to come into my room when I'm practicing?" he demanded.

I tried to apologize but in fact I felt stung. "I just needed to get my notebook. I'm sorry. I know you don't like it when I disrupt your meditation." He looked very angry and repeated himself.

I began getting pissed off and defensive. I made a nasty face and said, "Look at you, you say you're practicing compassion, but in the middle of it you treat me like dirt. Where is your compassion when it's needed the most?"

He was quiet. I walked out and closed the door. The whole day I felt tense and angry. When I got home later, we tried to patch things up but got into a huge fight instead. It ended by my screaming the last thing I ever wanted to hear myself sincerely call someone.

Granted, we argued about different things than your typical couple might, but the anger, fear, and grief were just as potent as with any couple. Power struggles, territoriality concerns, abandonment wounds, control issues—all the things that arise from a bad childhood—appeared within two months, just after our "honeymoon period" was ending. Even though we both strove for insight, peacefulness, and compassion, our practice manifested itself selectively. If anything, our practice might have forced our issues to the surface more dramatically and much earlier than in a conventional relationship because we were so intensely aware of every flicker of negative emotion. We were brave enough to confront the issue,

we began to believe that these outward modes actually expressed some inner truth.

knowing that an argument about who moved the plant to the other window was really a power struggle caused by not enough recognition as children. But even with our courage to be honest, with hours dedicated to cultivating communication skills, to try couples' therapy, to admit when we were wrong, to try to be caring—toward the end, this Buddhist relationship was depleting, not enriching, us.

I began to think, after three years of passionate loving and arguing we spent together, that having a Buddhist partner was irrelevant. The kind of growth Jasper and I needed is necessary with any mature couple. I began to think that spirituality was actually a bad impetus for a relationship, at least for me. It seemed that our self-perceptions as spiritual beings, as Buddhists, made our relationship worse.

It seemed that our self-perceptions as spiritual beings made our relationship worse.

Forcing ourselves to be "good Buddhists" was actually a façade, which covered our deeper anxieties and feelings. Things were out of balance. We'd be honest about less consequential things and blind to certain true vulnerabilities. At a subtle level we were perhaps using the fact that we were Buddhist to excuse ourselves from real respect, communication, listening, and love. Maybe we believed our Buddhist masks so much that we held each other to very high standards. When one of us would explode, the other was supposed to be a buddha, with infinite understanding and wisdom. And, just as Jasper was hiding from himself by sitting on the cushion, I was hiding from myself by not meditating.

To have a Buddhist boyfriend or not? Today, I think I had it wrong both ways when the debate was framed originally: It's not that one needs to have a spiritual partner to develop a good relationship, but rather a good relationship can be a springboard for developing one's self spiritually. Instead of Buddhism being the basis for relationship, it now seems to me that the fundamentals of relationship—love, care, kindness, respect, honesty—are the foundation of being Buddhist.

THE BACKWARD STEP

Paul W. Morris

"Given the cost of living, the ambient hypertension and the clatter-
ing grind, the decision to move to New York remains at least somewhat irrational, requiring a kind of quasi-religious commitment."

—Kurt Andersen, from "My First Year in New York,"
The New York Times Magazine, September 17, 2000

M Y KOAN BEGINS with a departure: I had to leave New York so that
I could return to it.

Manhattan never held much allure for me. Growing up and attending
school in rural New England, I always preferred bucolic spaciousness to
urban sprawl and could never reconcile the city's frenetic pace with my
own need for a sedate environment. I was an infrequent and reluctant visitor ever since getting lost as a child on the sidewalks of midtown. Sep-
arated from my parents in the hurtling immediacy of pedestrian traffic,
I panicked, feeling suffocated among the throngs of passersby, wondering if I'd be alone forever. Moments later, my father plucked me from the
torrent and I was safe, able to breathe again. After such a brush with loss,
I was in no hurry to return. But for the hordes of pilgrims journeying to
the city every year, New York's appeal is undeniable—it is the *uber-*
metropolis, the alpha and omega of cities, and their dream of this Mecca
is fulfilled once they make it their home.

I failed to understand this devotion and resisted moving to Manhattan
for many months after graduating college. I was, however, devoted to
my girlfriend and eventually moved one bitter January weekend to be

PAUL W. MORRIS, 28, IS A FREELANCE WRITER AND FORMER EDITOR AT *TRICYCLE: THE
BUDDHIST REVIEW* AND VIKING PENGUIN. HE LIVES IN MANHATTAN.

with her. My obstinacy matched her fervor for the city. We agreed that I wouldn't be long in New York, a year at most, then it was off to Asia, the West Coast, and graduate school, in that order. I longed to embody my undergraduate studies in sacred literature and live for a while on an island or atop a mountain, developing my practice without disruption before returning to the academy. At that early twenty-something, post-college crossroads, I believed myself capable of divining the entire course of my life,

> I believed myself capable of divining the entire course of my life.

certain that I not only knew the Path but that I was making progress on it. I kept friends and family and the city itself at bay by insisting that New York was not part of the equation, that it was just a detour, a distraction. This is the secret toll the city exacts from its inhabitants: reinforcing a false construct that serves as a barrier separating self from other.

Several obstacles conspired against me from the start. I blamed a low, entry-wage publishing salary and a high-priced, cramped upper–East Side rental for my early discontent. My work itself was fulfilling—editing spirituality and Beat-related titles—but the days were long and the weekends consumed with reading manuscripts that ranged from New Age *feng shui* manuals to Jack Kerouac's *Some of the Dharma*. I convinced myself that the job was the necessary balm to assuage the severity of New York life; if I couldn't be a monastic, then I would settle for being surrounded by the words of those who, if not monastics themselves, had some proximity to a more contemplative life than the one I knew.

Despite the small size of my apartment, I was able to carve out a little refuge for meditating. On the cushion, my *zafu*, I could be elsewhere, anywhere but New York, controlling my breathing as I sat quiet and still. Returning again and again to my breath when distracted by stray thoughts, I was able to come back to the moment, retreating twice a day for twenty minutes at a time. If the occasional sirens or dump trucks captured my attention, then they were just more noise contributing to my monkey mind—thousands of thoughts passing through my consciousness as quickly as they arose—and it was okay. Although my practice probably suffered from my not having a teacher, I sensed my meditation was improving and that was enough for me to continue.

Beyond the breath there is no control.

The subway was another story. The very act of commuting was physically and psychically exhausting. Crammed like cattle into cars that rumble along at industrial velocities, I would feel the pressure of more than mere bedrock weighing down upon me. Any progress I'd made on the cushion being still was gone in a blink, replaced by the imperative to *move*. My morning routine was as regimented as my sitting practice. I would rush to the subway, plunk down a dollar fifty, and shoot into the belly of Grand Central Station. There I would transfer for a crosstown train pumping me into the heart of Times Square before hopping on another downtown express that spit me out a few blocks from my office. On a good day, it would take me 40 minutes door-to-desk. On a bad one, it could take over an hour. If I synchronized the opening of subway car doors to align with the turnstile exits and went full-throttle out of the gates, I figured I could stay ahead of the wave of commuters crashing down behind me just enough to feel like I was in control.

Beyond the breath, though, there is no control. Everything is in constant flux, frustratingly elusive. Sometimes it was all I could do to filter out the kinetic thundering of the trains and forge a path ahead, shouldering my way through the crowds with total disregard for everyone else. I had to narrow my scope and increase my boundaries. Riding together, bumping elbows and stepping on toes, jostling back and forth, vying for a slippery handhold when hoping for a seat became futile, I was as inflexible as the next commuter, believing firmly she was invading my space or he was preventing me from getting to work on time. When

I caught my reflection in a greasy window, I saw tightness in my face and stress in my posture. By the time I arrived at my office cubicle, exhausted before the day had even begun, I was glad to have my own area to occupy however meager it was. I was relieved to be alone.

Living in New York City instilled in me the need for anonymity. I became adept at blocking out the incessant external stimuli, the countless images of suffering I encountered every day. I wore into the sidewalk an unnatural and unimaginative groove that afforded me the illusion of getting by, of coasting through the city, but my skin was thickening and my mind hardening. Pretty soon there was no room left for anything *other*. I never made eye contact. I didn't give to panhandlers. I would avoid the homeless sleeping half-naked on the sidewalks. Eventually, I didn't have to avoid them—I'd stopped noticing them altogether.

I awoke four years later to realize I'd been living in Manhattan intractably, cynically, and with convictions too strong for my own good. I resented New York for preventing me from living the life I'd always envisioned for myself. When out of sheer frustration I forfeited my job as a book editor, I held New York accountable for my intolerance. When I allowed my relationship with my girlfriend to gradually expire after five committed years, I blamed my apathy on New York. Not even the opportunity to work at a Buddhist magazine, where at midday our entire office sat in silent meditation with the phones off the hook, had been a panacea. My *zazen* practice disintegrated in the myriad twinkling distractions the city offered. I sought solace more and more frequently in the Manhattan nightlife, preferring the barstool to the zafu.

In New York, where what you do for a living takes precedence over how you live, my reply to the most frequently asked question, "What do

My zazen practice disintegrated in the myriad twinkling distractions the city offered.

you do?" invariably lead people to inquire, "Are you a Buddhist?" I began to doubt the pivot of my life and could not, in good conscience, respond to the latter question with a *yes*. I was saturated by the pervasiveness of spirituality in popular culture. It became increasingly difficult to distinguish between authentic and commercial intentions. From Brad Pitt's softness in *Seven Years in Tibet* to the *shunyata*-like teachings in *The Matrix's* Kung Fu sequences, spirituality had been appropriated by Hollywood and corporate America. Advertising companies used wisdom traditions to sell everything from automobiles to alarm clocks, while the publishing industry cashed in on the hybrid effect, linking mysticism with dating, sports, and even money. Surrounded by so much meaningfulness, it all ceased to mean anything.

Caught in the rush of overstimulation, I believed New York had infected me with its vanity and avarice. It became the perfect scapegoat, a repository for all my ill will, the root of my increasing callousness. Stripped of identity of job and relationship, I made up my mind: As the final act of self-inquiry, I would leave New York City.

But leaving can sometimes bring you back, to yourself and to your home, more balanced, less rigid, better equipped to begin confronting the prosaic hurdles that present themselves.

And coming home can change your mind in so many ways.

I returned to New York after volunteering abroad, to take a number of part-time jobs—at a bar, on a boat, in a store. I tried to live in the city, being more mindful of the moment. A new New York began to reveal itself, one I hadn't—couldn't have—known previously. I stepped backward, got a fresh vantage, and saw it as the perfect place for practice, a center of gravity amidst the tumult. I varied my commutes. I went the long way to work. In no particular rush, I let the crowds swallow me, and I wandered aimlessly. I discovered that opportunities to practice right livelihood were present everywhere, each obstacle and encounter a challenge to actualize the dharma. There was even practice on the subway.

Breathing in the surrounding negative energy of the train car, I would detach with compassion, exhaling a hope that everyone be more relaxed. I didn't shy away from eye contact either, instead considering it a chance to transmit a kind of photochemical loving-kindness.

Suddenly, I realized I had changed my mind about New York. I had become more flexible and consequently found an unexpected zeal for the city.

So I made it my home.

For me, *upaya* has its finest expression here. I was reminded of the city's skillful means while walking home late one night. Absorbed in the hail of my own internal chatter, I was startled by a car horn from an idling taxicab and looked up to meet the eyes of a driver motioning to his mouth, lips, and teeth, grinning like a mad prophet. I smiled automatically, unconsciously, not as a result of his gesture, but at the silent exchange itself, at his concern for the dour expression I must have been wearing as I ambled along. No words were spoken, and yet I understood his intention to be compassionate. Whereas once I would have heard the horn and tensed for a confrontation, ready to stand my ground and claim the space I occupied, I was immediately grateful for this dharma lesson, my own personal *udumbara* flower. I've used it as a wake-up call to others several times since.

The city is my teacher, my sangha, and my monastic cell.

It occurs to me sometimes how I could have left the city permanently, to an island, a mountain, or even the academy, with an abundance of space and time at my disposal to meditate in peace. But Manhattan is my island now: the best place to practice precisely because it is the worst place to practice. The city is my teacher. It is my sangha and my monastic cell, my adversity and refuge, rife with unabated suffering and unlimited potential joy. Like me, New York is full of contradictions, a place where I can exist, in the moment, on the zafu or on the subway, minding my breath as I take my time unraveling its koan.

Climbing with Tara

Ben Galland

I T WAS A CLASSIC HIGH SIERRA DAY in late August: warm sunshine, long days, and cool nights. I was up in the Tuolumne Meadows area backpacking with my mom. We camped at a lake at the base of the Mathes Crest rock formation. This rock formation rises straight up out of the ground about 1,500 feet and is sheer on both sides. It looks like a monolithic shark's fin—a really big piece of rock. My mom and I were doing a little climbing in the area, and today was a rest day for my mom. When I woke, I saw her doing her morning meditation, and I was inspired to do some sort of meditation for myself, too.

I decided to go climb the fin. I grabbed a little daypack and threw in some snacks and a water bottle. I didn't know how long it was going to take

I reached for another hold, but it broke off in my hand.

me, but I figured I would be gone for just a few hours. I headed up the hill from the lake to the base of the cliff. There I stood, with no ropes, at the base of this 1,500-foot monolith thinking to myself, good morning. I had climbed without ropes before so I knew what I was getting myself into. I had to really be in the present moment and not think about anything else but the handhold I was grabbing and the foothold I was stepping on. I practiced some rounds of controlled, deep breathing to get

BEN GALLAND, 29, IS WORKING ON A VIDEO ABOUT EXTREME SPORTS AND DHARMA.

in my body. I had had some experience with meditation from growing up close to a Zen center and having a mother who meditated every day. As a little boy, my mom occasionally encouraged me to meditate in the mornings before I went to school.

I began to climb up the cliff, grabbing onto a handhold and squeezing it gently enough to hold on but not too hard as to clutch it. With every step I took and hold I grabbed, I would take a deep breath and try to relax. I slowly made my way up the cliff using the movement of each hold as a stretch for my body. I would put one foot way out to the left and then would sit on it for a second and stretch out in that position for a breath cycle. This technique made me slow down and helped me relax.

"Let your thoughts be like clouds, and let them pass across the sky with the wind."

I slowly made my way up this apron of rock with the sun shining warmly on my back. The wind blew gently, and the air was fresh and crisp. I continued to follow the cracks, little paths to the top of the cliff. After about an hour of climbing, I really began to feel the exposure of this piece of rock. I was about a thousand feet off the ground when I got to some looser rock on the route. I had to slow down even more because I didn't want to grab anything that could come off in my hands and send me whipping over backward to the ground. *O-o-o-k-a-a-a-y*, deep breath out. I was beginning to get a little scared. Everything I was grabbing or stepping on was loose, and I realized that my holds could slide out from under me at any second. The higher I got, the worse the rock got. With 1,400 feet of air below me, I should have just turned back, but I was so close to the top that I really wanted to just get there.

I reached for another hold, but it broke off in my hand. Fortunately, I had tested the hold before putting all my weight on it. I took the hold and threw it down the cliff below me. I watched it fall for about 800 feet and then blow up into a million pieces as it smashed into the side of the cliff below. I was definitely scared at this point, and I began to freeze up.

Everywhere I looked for a hold the rock was crappy. The granite was grainy and old, what climbers call "'chaossy.'" But I was only fifty feet away from the summit, and I really didn't want to turn around. I was thinking that if I got to the top, I could climb down a safer way.

I grabbed a few more awful holds and threw them off the cliff, trying to clean out the rock from where I had just removed the hold, but it all just turned to sand. I would have to make do with what I had and pick my holds with great attention. Some of the holds I grabbed were loose, but I just eased onto them and didn't put a lot of weight on them. I grabbed for the last hold and pulled myself up onto the summit block of the shark's fin.

The view and the exposure were both spectacular and terrifying. I usually love to feel like I am sitting on top of the world, but not when the world could crumble down from underneath me. I looked down over to the lake below, and I could see my mother still doing her meditation. I then realized that I was in trouble. There was no other way down. I looked off the other side of the cliff, and there was nothing but very steep, overhanging cliff. The only way down was to go back the way I came. I was not happy but I was in no hurry. I began to pray like my mom had shown me as a kid, for when times got tough or just to say thanks for what we had.

I got into a lotus position on the summit of this 1,500-foot pillar of granite, at 10,000 feet in the High Sierra back country. I took a deep breath. I looked to the west and let the sun shine into my eyes and warm my face. I felt a breeze blow against my face and stir my hair. Then I remembered a teaching that a Buddhist teacher once gave me when I was practicing meditation a few years back. "Let your thoughts be like clouds, and let them pass across the sky with the wind." I breathed deeply

I asked Tara, the goddess of compassionate action, to come into my life and help me.

to let go of the horrible fear that was churning in my stomach. Thoughts were running through my head, even though I was totally safe at the present moment where I was sitting. I would have a moment of clarity, then I would stress again about my situation, and then I would catch myself and try to breathe deeply. I tried to let the wind blow my frantic thoughts across the sky and out of my mind. I knew that I needed to be totally present, calm, and grounded if I were going to make it to the bottom, so I sat in meditation until I got there—and sat, and sat some more.

The sitting helped but it wasn't complete. Suddenly, I flashed back to my mom's altar, and I saw her statues and images of deities. I asked Tara, the goddess of compassionate action, to come into my life and help me out. "Help me down off this mountain and help me to focus and help me let go of my fears right now so that I can be totally present for the descent," I prayed.

I closed my eyes and took more breaths, and then I saw an image of the goddess Tara hovering over my body and the mountain, and she was smiling at me. As the wind blew and I took more deep breaths, her smile began to fill my belly with a warm, fuzzy feeling. I took another breath from this place in my stomach and as I exhaled, I began to smile myself. With every breath I took I began to smile more and more until my smile stretched across my face and I began laughing to myself.

whether she really exists is not important; Tara saved my life.

It was at that point that I felt ready for the descent; my mind was settled and calm. It felt like I was dreaming as I moved over to the edge of this 1,500-foot cliff and turned around backward to climb down. My feet went right to the solid parts of the rock and so did my hands. I didn't even have to think; I felt like I was a river, flowing down the side of the mountain, around and over the rocks in the way. One foot behind the other and one hand behind the other. I kept breathing and moving down, and before I knew it, I was through the roughest section of loose rock. I got back to the ground and was still smiling. My face hurt from the intensity of the smiling, which I had been doing the whole way down and hadn't noticed. On the solid earth, I was so happy to still be alive and in the present moment.

I'm not sure what would have happened if I hadn't taken time to calm my mind. But the one thing I do know is that Tara and meditation gave me serenity in the midst of a very scary situation that could have been fatal. Without a calm mind, maybe Tara wouldn't have been able to appear, to help me become that river flowing down the side of the cliff. Nevertheless, as a result of that experience, my mindfulness practice and belief in Tara is stronger than before. Whether she really exists is not important; Tara saved my life.

RUNNING AS MEDITATION

David Zuniga

M Y SPIRITUAL PATH as a runner has revealed itself gradually. Like many in my generation, I have always been active in sports. As a child I played soccer and baseball. In middle school I began studying Tae Kwon Do. In high school I played football. In college I played rugby, worked as a lifeguard, and earned my black belt. Up until my senior year in college, I saw running as mere conditioning for other sports. But that year, looking for new athletic challenges, I joined the cross-country team.

I soon discovered that I was out of my league. Though I was athletic, I was contending against people who had been running competitively for many years. My first race taught me a lesson I would never forget. My ego caused me to line up near the front, and I foolishly tried to stay with the front-runners. But the first two miles at a 4:30 pace destroyed me. My entire body was wracked with pain; I felt nauseated and weak. I continued to go slower and slower. I ran my third mile in ten minutes, and soon I was in last place. Some of the spectators even laughed at me.

I was dejected and about to quit when I heard a runner from another team say, "Don't quit, you can do it. Only two miles to go." Though he was my rival and much stronger, he stayed with me, stride for stride, for the next two miles. Without him, I have no doubt that I would have quit my very first collegiate race. That would have been humiliating. But he was patient and compassionate and refused to leave my side.

DAVID ZUNIGA, 30, IS A STUDENT OF BUDDHISM AND CHRISTIANITY IN DIVINITY SCHOOL.

Because we were going so slowly, I was able to regain some of my strength. As we entered the stadium, with only 400 meters left, I heard the roar of the crowd. I saw my teammates and coach frantically waving me on. Suddenly I remembered that my new friend and I were the last two runners. Embarrassed and desperate not to finish in last place, I frantically surged ahead with my last ounce of strength and passed my friend at the finish. The crowd cheered. My teammates congratulated me for recovering my energy and passing him at the end. But I knew the truth.

where the mind goes, the body will follow.

The truth was I never would have finished the race if not for the runner on the other team. Without his patience and compassion I would have quit after three miles. My ego made me insecure and drove me to cutthroat competition against someone who had helped me. He easily could have beaten me if he wanted to, but winning was not so important to him. Though I technically did not finish last, the better athlete had not won. I was silent for the entire four-hour bus ride home.

Humbled, I continued running. After college I ran several half marathons, then full marathons, and eventually I moved up in distance to ultramarathons. A marathon distance race is 26.2 miles, so an ultramarathon is anything longer than that. Common ultramarathon distances are 50 kilometers (31 miles), 50 miles, 100 kilometers (62 miles), and 100 miles. There are many races that go for even longer distances, and some offer other additional challenges such as running through the Rocky Mountains or the Sahara Desert. The longest event I have completed is 100 kilometers.

People run for many of the same reasons they participate in other sports. Some people run for fitness. Many run for ego gratification. In our country, we often praise the value of competition. Competition challenges us; it forces us to do our best, to give it our all. We have all heard these clichés. But I reject the notion that competition is good. Competition is fueled by the ego and immerses the athlete in an endless cycle of *samsara*. If I were to run only because I wanted to beat someone else, then it would be better that I not run at all. I run for the same reason that I meditate: because it is my nature, and because it is part of my path.

Paavo Nurmi, the great Finnish runner who won nine Olympic gold medals in distance running, once observed, "Mind is everything. All that I am, I am because of my mind." Running, like traditional meditation, helps me to train and understand my mind.

Running keeps me radically attentive to the here and now of existence.

Where the mind goes, the body will follow. This is my personal mantra that I chant while running. My body is mere flesh and blood, a source of *dukkha*, of suffering. Running is the spiritual practice in which I immerse myself in suffering. This voluntary suffering may sound masochistic, but allowing myself to suffer allows me to train my mind and overcome suffering so that I may serve other sentient beings.

The fruits of my running are many. Running disciplines my mind to be constantly aware and yet also tranquil. In an ultramarathon, my mind must be like a cat: attentive and focused to the smallest of details. I must constantly monitor my pace, my caloric intake, my fluid intake, my electrolyte levels, my equipment, my body, and especially my mind. As a race progresses and my body encounters new dimensions of suffering, my mind must resist temptation and remain focused.

Running keeps me radically attentive to the here and now of existence. Ann Trason, one of the greatest ultramarathon runners ever, was once asked how she was able to win so many grueling races. She responded, "I do it tree to tree." Focusing on the here and now keeps one from becoming lost. It dissolves pain and keeps the mind safe from destructive emotions. Awakening to the here and now also cultivates sensitivity and allows the runner to perceive the subtle beauty inherent in all objects and sentient beings. It keeps all things fresh and new. Every tree, every rock, every speck of dust is a source of wonder and mystery, even when we have run the same path countless times.

But my mind must be in perfect balance. While radically aware, I must also be in a state of equanimity. During extreme running, the mind experiences many emotions, anger, fear, exhilaration. But these are just fleeting mental states that lead to suffering. Even becoming overly excited or "pumped up" can prove to be destructive.

Through running, I learn that all things are fleeting and everything is subject to change. One moment I feel strong and healthy, as if I could run forever, but in the next moment my body can be wracked with horrible pain, and each step is agony. Everything changes; there is nothing to cling to. I must embrace all states of running with calm acceptance.

Embracing change fosters patience, the lifeblood of running. Patience is the fuel that empowers the runner to travel mile after mile alone and in silence. Patience is the teacher that helps one run wisely.

Running teaches humility. No matter how hard I train, there will always be many who are faster, who can run farther. The suffering and obstacles that other runners have overcome amazes me, and I know that my own running pales in comparison. I can take no credit for any of my running. Anything in running that I have accomplished is a result of infinite sacrifices by countless sentient beings.

Awareness, equanimity, patience, and humility naturally create compassion and love. I have been blessed in countless ways through the compassion of others while running. My prayer is that my running makes me more compassionate. If it doesn't, then I have lost the most valuable lesson that running teaches.

Running naturally lends itself to Buddhist practice; it has been the primary form of meditation for some Japanese and Tibetan orders for over 1,200 years. Only a select few of the Japanese Tendai monks

running teaches humility.

of Mount Hiei are allowed to undergo the *sennichi kaihogyo* (1,000-day marathon), which spans seven years. For the first three years, the monks complete a yearly ritual of running 24.8 miles every day for 100 consecutive days. This athletic feat is made even more amazing when one considers that a traditional marathon is 26.2 miles, only 1.4 miles longer than what the Tendai monks run every day during their running meditation term. During the fourth and fifth years this running period increases to 200 consecutive days per year. In the sixth year their running meditation period drops back to 100 consecutive days, but their distance per day increases to 37.2 miles. In the seventh and final year of training, these monks again run for 200 consecutive days. For the first 100 days they run for an amazing 52 miles per day, and for the last 100 days they again complete 24.8 miles per day. The only stops they make during their runs are at stations of worship for various Buddhist deities and Tendai patriarchs. They eat a vegetarian diet and average four hours of sleep a night. The *lung-gompa* runners of Tibet are renowned for their ability to cover vast distances at a very fast pace for several days and nights without stopping. Eyewitnesses have attested that these monks run so fast that they actually appear to be flying. Like the Tendai monks, the lung-gompa runners eschew any modern athletic conveniences; they run only in traditional monastic robes.

Running rescues me from this misguided notion of existence.

Such extreme feats may seem odd and excessive; some Buddhists might protest that Siddhartha Gautama found enlightenment through the middle way. But I think these athletic endeavors demonstrate *upaya*, the skillful means of the dharma to manifest itself in every facet of existence. The Tendai monks believe that they can only accomplish their death-defying physical activities because they are following the bodhisattva path. They achieve complete mastery of their minds and bodies for the sake of all sentient beings. By conquering unimaginable physical pain, they are revered as living buddhas and, like Shakyamuni, prove that dukkha can be overcome.

To run with any degree of skill one must focus on breathing. In *Zen Mind, Beginner's Mind*, Shunryu Suzuki describes the process of breathing in meditation:

When we practice zazen our mind always follows our breathing. When we inhale, the air comes into the inner world. When we exhale, the air goes out to the outer world. The inner world is limitless, and the outer world is also limitless. We say "inner world" or "outer world," but actually there is just one whole world. In this limitless world, our throat is like a swinging door. The air comes in and goes out like someone passing through a swinging door. If you think, "I breathe," the "I" is extra. There is no you to say "I." What we call "I" is just a swinging door that moves when we inhale and when we exhale. It just moves; that is all. When your mind is pure and calm enough to follow this movement, there is nothing: no "I," no world, no mind nor body; just a swinging door.

Breath is the essence of running. Breathing carelessly wastes precious oxygen and forces the runner to stop. By watching the breath properly, one will have a natural, relaxed pace and feel like the lung-gompa runners sailing effortlessly across the high, grassy plains of Tibet. The words *lung-gompa* convey this: *lung* denotes the elementary state of air, and *gom* means meditation. So the lung-gompa runner is one who completely masters breath meditation.

Breath is the essence of running.

Even more importantly, as we follow our breath in running, the self-imposed barriers, which are a product of delusional thinking and lead to dichotomous conceptions of existence, dissolve. Much of the time I tend to focus on myself. I foolishly act as if I am a discrete, individual entity, and I worry about my own selfish concerns. But running rescues me from this misguided notion of existence. As I run, I naturally focus on the oxygen moving in and out of my body. I feel my diaphragm expand and contract, expand and contract—over and over again in an endless pattern of repetition for mile after mile after mile. Slowly all suffering disappears. Pleasure and pain are fleeting sensations. There is no longer a sense of

"I"; there is simply running. For a few precious moments I am at peace with all sentient beings as I feel the deep and powerful presence of existence flowing, unimpeded, through me.

DREAM A BETTER DREAM

Cameron Warner

BEFORE I TRAVELED TO NEPAL, my Tibetan teacher in New York City, the Venerable Lama Pema Wangdak, told me he had a lot of faith in me. He said that even though my experiences would probably not meet with my preconceptions about Tibetan Buddhist monasteries, I would return transformed rather than disillusioned. I was thankful that Lama Pema had warned me that something unexpected was going to happen. That something happened when I found myself, seemingly without reason, invited by His Holiness the Sakya Trizin, who is the head of Sakya lineage of Tibetan Buddhism, to go to Lumbini, the Buddha's birthplace, where the Great Prayer Festival *(Monlam)* was taking place.

Thousands and thousands of candles were radiating into the night.

I was fortunate enough to actually travel with Sakya Trizin, his family, his monk attendants, and two other Westerners in a procession of cars that got a military escort into Lumbini. People were waving Buddhist flags along the road, and there were big banners welcoming His Holiness. All the pageantry and attention made me feel like I was some sort of prince, rather than just a lucky nobody who happened to be included in His Holiness's entourage.

When we got to the monastery of His Eminence Chobgye Trichen Rinpoche in Lumbini, His Holiness's attendants said they wanted to find

CAMERON WARNER, 25, GRADUATE STUDENT IN BUDDHISM, IS A STUDENT OF HIS HOLINESS SAKYA TRIZIN.

a nice hotel for me. They thought I was crazy to pass this up when I insisted on staying with the monks in their tents. I explained that I came here to get to know the monks better, not to isolate myself in relatively luxurious surroundings. After I found the tent-grounds, I managed to convince a few of the monks to let me stay with them. That evening, I found myself drinking soup with some monks in a large tent built by the side of the road, which served as a temporary restaurant during the prayer festival. I was the only Westerner in sight, surrounded by monks in their burgundy robes and a few lay Tibetans as well.

As I looked up at the stars through the tent's opening, I felt a rush of exhilaration. I felt like I had traveled back in time to a long-lost culture. I wanted to stay in Nepal for years, not just days. Not a word of English was to be heard anywhere. I ate *thukpa*, Tibetan soup, with the monks and thought, "This is an indescribable feeling. I couldn't be happier."

wow, I get to do this again!

After dinner, we walked over to the Buddha's birthplace. Thousands and thousands of candles lit by the three thousand monks and nuns were glowing around the entire prayer center, radiating into the night. Crowds of men and women robed in maroon and yellow were circumambulating clockwise around the birth site. Off in the corner I saw a group of monks debating in the traditional style, slapping their hands after each emphatic point. I imagined I had been dropped into a monastery in Tibet before the Chinese Invasion. Totally in awe, I thought again, "This is the greatest experience of my life."

The second day, I prayed with the monks in Tibetan for eight hours straight. The monks were so excited that I could (barely) read Tibetan that they helped me along during the prayers. Everyone wanted to teach me how to speak Tibetan. That night we had dinner, a break, and then soup in the tent again. I thought again about how amazing and otherworldly it seemed. Then we went back to the prayer center and circumambulated again. I thought, "Wow, I get to do this *again!*"

But when I woke up the third day my legs were very sore from sitting all day long on hard ground without a meditation cushion. My back hurt as I prayed with the monks for another eight hours. Again we had dinner in the restaurant tent and circumambulated all evening. When I woke up the next morning, my legs were incredibly sore from walking all evening, and my back was killing me from keeping it straight during the eight hours of praying. After loosening my limbs a little and having breakfast, I went and sat

How could these prayers have any effect on the world?

down at the prayer site for another eight hours of praying. My throat began to get sore and my voice was hoarse. I started to feel really tired. That night we had dinner, then the soup, followed by more circumambulating. I was starting to get a little bored. I thought, "We did this yesterday."

The fourth day I woke up, and it was the same thing. I sat down on the hard ground again and prayed with the monks all day. I noticed my throat was getting hoarse from all the praying. I felt the same combination of pain and exhaustion in my body, as if I had just run a marathon. That night we had dinner, and circumambulated again. I was starting to get bored, lonely, and depressed. I thought, "Haven't we done this already?" Soon, I started to lose track of how long I had been in Lumbini and when we would leave.

Suddenly it wasn't a magical experience anymore. I realized the thukpa was Ramen noodles, just like the ones I could get at the grocery stores in America. All the cook did in the tent was open up the little plastic bags and dump it all in boiling water. Some of the monks had gone through the trouble to preopen soup packages back at the monastery, and they brought their stash of extra seasoning packets to Lumbini. They were kind enough to share the wealth with me, and I appreciated it enormously. But I had already become skeptical of the entire Monlam. The hundreds of times we walked, literally in circles, began to lose meaning. All the praying seemed pointless, too. I thought, "How could these prayers have any effect on the world if the monks and nuns who say them are so unmindful that they walk all over the beautiful flowers here and trample them to death? They aren't even using the proper toilet area and there are human feces all over the place. And why aren't all these people doing something constructive back in the towns near their monasteries to help all the poor Indian and Nepalese people who invited them into their countries instead? Wouldn't that lead to more peace than sitting and praying all day?"

I had come to a real impasse. I thought, "What am I doing here? What's the point? How silly am I that I thought the first day this was the greatest thing, and this was what I'd always wanted to see." I felt miserable, and even worse when I remembered that I'd charged this whole trip to my credit card. It felt like a waste of time. I decided not to go pray that day but to do something else, although I had no idea what. I began feeling sorry for myself that I was here between Thanksgiving and Christmas and my family was so far away. The monks had decorated everything with bright, colored lights that were, in fact, Christmas lights. Some strings had little speakers that played a fifteen-second jingle from ten different Christmas songs. I tried to explain, in broken Tibetan, to one of the monks who Rudolph the Red-Nosed Reindeer was. I wanted to connect with someone who understood how I was feeling, but it was a hopeless endeavor from the start. I was terribly homesick.

what am i doing here?

The next day when I was sitting around, not knowing what I was going to do, I noticed that some new students had arrived. They had come for a special ceremony. I saw them going in and out of the monastery, so I thought, "I've never even been inside; I wonder what's in there." When I wandered upstairs, I found myself surrounded by a swarm of busy monks running everywhere. Then I saw His Holiness's son and wife walk by, and I realized that I was in the private quarters of his family. Just as I was about to leave in embarrassment, one of the monks grabbed me and said, "Would you like some tea? Oh, you don't have any tea; we'll get you some tea." Then he sped off.

I couldn't leave at that point because I was obliged to drink the tea. As I was waiting, His Holiness's wife, Dagmo Kusho, began asking me all kinds of questions about myself. She was so kind to me and glad that I had come to the Monlam. One of the monks arranged for me to have an audience with His Holiness in order to learn more about the Monlam. During the audience, I started to ask His Holiness small questions about the prayers. Somehow His Holiness sensed my skepticism. He started telling me about the prayer festival, why he has all the monks and nuns travel here, and how he felt these prayers were helping people around the world. I can say it was very moving to hear him talk about it. I began to understand that there was much more to the Monlam than I had ever imagined.

As he spoke, I began to feel moved by his sincerity and heartfelt faith in the prayer festivals' efficacy and necessity. His Holiness was able to see past all of the superficial things that had been bothering me to the beautiful underlying purpose.

something changed in me and I started to see differently.

Something changed in me and I started to see it differently also. It wasn't about being in an exotic location, or the behavior of the monks. It was about sincerely and selflessly devoting a few days of one's life to the benefit of others. It was a subtle but powerful statement about the nature of true happiness and true peace. When I walked out of his room, I felt that I had changed, and that the world had changed. I could see everything in a different light.

At that moment, I remembered the words of my teacher Lama Pema back in the States, and I felt like I understood what he was talking about. I was not going to go home with a negative view of Buddhism and Tibetan refugee culture because it did not match up with my expectations. I let my expectations go, and I focused on seeing and experiencing the prayer festival from His Holiness's point of view. Through his eyes, the festival was the most fundamental and profound way to change the world. For the rest of the prayer festival, I regretted feeling sorry for myself and felt excited for each day that was left.

I realized that my first view, the naïve excitement, is just as empty as the second view, disillusionment and negativity. There is something past those two extremes that each of us can get to if we have the right mindset. Lama Pema says,

> The world around us is just a dream, no more real than the dreams we have when we are asleep. Often we dream about the same people, the same places as when we are awake. The difference is that when we are asleep we have no control over our actions. We have no control over whether the dream is happy or sad. When we are awake, we do have a certain amount of control over how we perceive our environment and ourselves. So when we are awake, we should dream a better dream.

My experience at the prayer festival showed me that a happy life is really that simple.

Ordinary Awakening

Jessica Morey

T HE INSIGHT MEDITATION SOCIETY (IMS) rests in the farm hills of western Massachusetts. The surrounding forests and abandoned fields are crisscrossed by crumbling stone walls, home to moss and to squirrels. The main building, a red brick mansion with tall white columns on the portico, was built by a local aristocrat. It had later become home to Christian monks, who added a chapel, which is now a meditation hall. In place of pews are rows of over a hundred meditation cushions, and on the altar sits a bronze Buddha. In the elegant ballroom adjacent to the hall, two stained-glass windows remain from the time of the monks. I often did slow walking meditation between one image of Jesus supplicating to God and another of his comforting the disciples on his last night. He is the image of compassion, a true bodhisattva. My anxious mind was frequently comforted by these images during walking meditations, sometimes aware of just the pad of my foot as it made contact with the polished wooden floor, in one moment aware of the whole leg filling and emptying of pressure, then in another moment lost in thought, and then angry at myself for my lack of concentration. I often prayed, "Please help me through this journey of mind. Please uplift me from the spiral of my thoughts."

> HOW can watching a breath come and go be claimed by any tradition?

JESSICA MOREY, 2 I, IS A JUNIOR IN COLLEGE STUDYING ENVIRONMENTAL ENGINEERING.

The stained-glass windows reminded me of my Roman Catholic upbringing. I am sometimes accused of deserting the Church by practicing "Buddhist" meditation. *Vipassana*, or the insight meditation tradition, came to IMS from Burma and is said to have been taught by the Buddha himself, yet vipassana meditation is nondenominational. How can watching a breath come and go or watching a thought arise and pass away be claimed by any tradition? Still, the few stone and wooden Buddha figures in the halls and corners of IMS, smiling serenely at me, reminded me that awakening is possible.

Vipassana meditation is a technique for awakening to the here and now. I meditated, for example, on a dry twig, its form becoming exquisite by bare attention. Look at the curve, and how the offshoot meets; how perfect, how magical. The closely examined form brought me to tears. If only I could see everything in the world with such attention, every person, drop of rain, insect, and breath with this kind of wonder and amazement.

Seeing the extraordinary in the ordinary is what I practiced on retreat. This is why I took a term off from my sophomore year of college to sit twelve hours a day in silence rather than hike the Himalayas or backpack through Europe. I wanted to learn what my prestigious education wasn't teaching me: to pay attention, to be present, to be alive, and especially, to begin to hold myself, my mind, and my experience with reverence.

seeing the extraordinary in the ordinary is what I practiced on retreat.

Vipassana meditation is considered by some to be one of the driest techniques. There are no koans to analyze, no deities to visualize, nothing to achieve. The only altered state vipassana meditators seek is to be awake to our lives rather than half-asleep, as most people normally go through our lives. Vipassana meditation is very ordinary. One attempts to be with whatever experience is arising in the body and mind. What is sound? What is pain and physical sensation? What is a thought? What is it to be alive? Who am I? But vipassana is not an analytical, mental exploration. Practicing meditation one quickly comes to realize the limitations of discursive thought. Understanding comes from direct experience, from simply watching what is happening in the moment. Whole worlds are created and destroyed sitting on the cushion; true loves meet, marry, and divorce; children are begotten; books written; Nobel prizes awarded. More amazing is what can unravel while sitting in disciplined silence.

Difficult emotional habits, like tangled knots, undo themselves in the space of silent awareness. We, the meditators, simply bear witness until our "selves" too are undone.

> ı wanted to learn what my prestigious education wasn't teaching me.

When I arrived at IMS during that term of my sophomore year, it was with joy to see the familiar faces of the staff. IMS had become my spiritual home after seven years of young-adult retreats. I was a little apprehensive, though, since the Three-Month, as everyone called it, was like the boot camp of retreats. No short half-hour sits followed periods of relaxation. Instead, I would be meditating twelve hours a day without breaks, and without talking. Still, here I was in this beautiful setting with nothing to do but breathe. No tests, no engineering problem sets, no papers, no deadlines, no small talk to make. In fact, we were asked to keep total silence, which included not calling home, writing letters, reading books, or even journaling. With no obligations whatsoever, what could be easier than watching my breath? By the third day of the retreat, I'd have answered: *Just about anything!*

The first few days of the retreat my mind flew everywhere. I couldn't follow two consecutive breaths. My mind was lost, first doubting that I should have even come here, then planning retreats for the next five years of my life, then wondering what was for lunch. My biggest preoccupation was judging the hundred other meditators: "Why am I the only person under thirty-five here?... I'm practically the only person who's not retired... I wish I had clothes as cool as that woman.... Why does that guy need so many cushions?" and on and on, like constant talk radio that I couldn't turn off. Realizing how judgmental I was and how much I reacted with aversion, I turned my judgments toward myself and began to mentally beat myself up about it.

The meditation teachers had warned us that the mind was likely to be unfocused in the beginning as we made the transition from the speed of daily life. Indeed, the first insight I experienced was how much I think, how much the mind flits around without my even noticing. Although it seemed like I was thinking more when I meditated than at other times, really I was just becoming aware of how much discursive thinking my mind continually creates. I accepted this for the first few days thinking, "Okay, this is normal. The mind is like a little puppy that needs to be trained." But when I was still spinning off on the fifth day, I decided that I must be the worst meditator in the room, that I'd never get it, and that there was something intrinsically wrong with me. I redoubled my efforts to stay with the breath.

I decided that I must be the worst meditator in the room.

Ironically, that very striving became the obstacle. I tried so hard that my jaw ached. My breathing became tight and shallow. It became difficult for me to even feel the sensations of the breath in my belly or at the tip of my nose. My meditation teacher, with whom I had a short interview every couple of days, recognized my struggle and the suffering it was causing me. He encouraged me to go for a walk around the pond, or play with the dogs down the street, or draw. He encouraged me to be happy and make myself at home, to be gentle with myself, to relax. "You can't meditate when the mind is tight and constricted; there's no space for understanding to arise," he told me.

I took my teacher's advice. I walked in the woods, trying to be totally present and aware and trying desperately to be awed and inspired by everything around me, by the ferns yellowing, lichen-covered rocks, sunsets and late flowers, by falling leaves, the beauty of a New England autumn. But I wasn't feeling awed by ordinariness. I was feeling constricted and detached, not in flow with the world's great cosmic dance, unable to be touched.

Then, I noticed that there was one time of day my mind felt at ease, during the last meditation period of the day. We would do a *metta* chant and meditation. Metta is the Pali word for loving-kindness. The Buddha taught thousands of types of meditation; 84,000 types, they say. Four of these are the *Brahma Viharas*, which translates as the *abodes of the gods*, that is, the best states of mind one can attain. These are loving-kindness, compassion, sympathetic joy, and equanimity. They are often considered the juicy practices that can be added to the dry vipassana. The basic instruction for each one is to repeat three or four phrases that convey the meaning of the intention, directing them toward someone, usually beginning with yourself, then moving on to a benefactor, a dear friend, a neutral person, someone you have problems with, and finally allowing the feelings of loving-kindness, compassion, or joy to spread to all beings.

The usual phrases for metta meditation are, "May you/I be happy and peaceful. May you/I be safe and protected. May you/I be healthy and strong. May you/I take care of your/myself happily while living on this earth." I started to play with the phrases to find ones that worked best for me, that aroused the feeling of true kindness, friendliness, and well-wishing. The phrases that arose were, "May I be happy *exactly* as I am. May I be free from all striving and self-judgment. May my life be filled with joy and ease." Occasionally I threw in, "May I love myself completely."

When I was doing metta meditation I could allow my mind to relax, finally. Even if I got distracted I would say all the things that had bothered me during the day, like, "May I be happy even if I get distracted and have no concentration." I'd often begin with forgiveness meditation and a meditation on why I am worthy of love, thinking

That very striving became the obstacle.

about the good things I've done or my good qualities to arouse a sense of appreciation and kindness toward myself. This kind of practice was such a relief after a day of mental self-flagellation.

When I told my teacher about this experience, he encouraged me to do more metta meditation, to switch to metta when I felt like I was drowning in self-judgment, despair, and worthlessness. He also encouraged me to explore my feelings of worthlessness. Where did they come from? What were some of their causes? Family, religion, society, childhood? Both of these suggestions came as a shock to me. Wasn't meditation about being completely stuck in the awareness of the breath and somewhere hidden in the inhalation was the truth, the point of life, the ultimate nature of reality? His redirection seemed radical, but I did it.

When I allowed myself to think about my feelings of worthlessness, memories began to flood my mind connected to my Catholic upbringing: the fact that women aren't worthy to be priests, that women are the reason for the fall of all humans from the garden of Eden. I thought about my culture: how media tells me that if I'm not stick-thin I'm worthless, that I have little worth as a woman outside of my sexual appeal to men. Even being academically successful in high school there was always the struggle for college admissions, then GPAs, then jobs, because we are replaceable. We have to fight to succeed because someone else can always take our place; we are not unique, not necessary to the universe. We have no intrinsic worth…. Wow, no wonder I feel worthless! There is a whole lifetime of conditioning to make my mind turn that way.

So I began to feel compassion for myself, for this poor girl trying to become a woman but not quite sure that's what she wants to be, in a culture that doesn't teach us how to be happy. Through awareness, I stepped out of identification with my own conditioned thought process. This feeling of compassion spread to my mother and friends and to all women on earth dealing with many of the same issues. Then the feeling expanded to all humans struggling in life—everyone struggles just to be alive. I began to do only metta meditation throughout the day. I explored sending loving-kindness toward different objects, like water, rocks,

wow, no wonder i feel worthless! There is a whole lifetime of conditioning to make my mind turn that way.

plants, and the earth. Metta is such a powerfully connecting practice that it allowed me to feel awed by the sunset, the flowers and the moss, as I had longed to in the weeks before. My mind felt spacious, my heart light.

I felt like I could never again get caught in a thought, an anger, or a depression.

I began to do metta for the constant critic in my mind. I started seeing the absurdity of my mind's ranting and the amusement of my self-judgments. I stopped taking myself so seriously. There seemed to be something bigger; a safety net embracing all of this experience, so that fundamentally there was nothing to worry about. In some way these passing experiences of joy, sorrow, grief, worthlessness, and pride, were pretend, like a costume party of emotions.

Metta began to permeate almost all moments of my days. After six weeks I began to do my own blend of vipassana-metta meditation. I felt a sense of loving-kindness toward each moment, toward each sensation, thought, and emotion. Eventually, there didn't seem to be much of a difference between awareness and metta practice because loving meant giving something my full attention and accepting it completely just as it is. Metta is mindfulness.

Metta-mindfulness embraced the second six weeks of the retreat. I practiced being gentle with myself, going for walks, running, drinking tea, examining the new flower arrangements each day, watching the sun rise and set, eating too much, feeling rage, annoyance, frustration, balancing rocks, taking a step, breathing. After having such a spacious experience, I felt like I could never again get caught in a thought, an anger, or a depression. How could I possibly ever return to a state of non-mindfulness?

At the end of the retreat, I went home for Christmas with my family. I kept a sense of balance and space for a few days, but it was a constant struggle. I was shell-shocked jumping from a world of simplicity and deep practice into the materialism of an American Christmas and a world where people weren't striving at every moment to cultivate love and attention. The noise generated from talking and the harshness of the outside world assaulted my senses. I longed for the cocoon of the IMS retreat and felt uncertain of how to live mindfully, how to maintain in the "real" world the peace I had found.

Going back to college was even more challenging. I didn't feel like I fit in. I would sit in class learning about electronic systems and take tests that students would cry over. I'd wonder how they could be so serious about it. I had a hard time putting my heart into studies, feeling like they were a joke after having spent three months searching for the meaning of life and intimately considering the truth of my own impermanence. After trying so hard to realize the concept of no-self, here I was building my Self up again with my grades and activities, and even, to my dismay, reifying my sense of self by talking about my retreat, which was a novelty and hot topic among my college friends.

I saw the effects of the retreat in my college life at a subtle level.

Though I no longer visit the divine abodes of metta and mindfulness as often as I did in retreat, I saw the effects of the retreat in my college life at a subtle level. Practice takes a more active form in my daily college life, in the subjects I choose to study, and in the activities where I put energy, in keeping the precepts, a nonharming moral code of body and speech, and in relationships. I practice mindful listening and speaking and loving in action. Though I miss my consistent ability to be open, gentle, and joyful on retreat, I realize now that college life is just as rich a place for practicing metta and vipassana as at IMS. I'm beginning to think that awakening is not about an ecstatic state of enlightenment in some idyllic location but is about the ordinary moment right here and right now. Taking three months out of school to discover this was the best semester I've ever had.

WINNING OVER DEPRESSION

Claudia Heiman

I WAS BORN IN 1971, the youngest of four children of middle-class American parents in Needham, Massachusetts, a suburb of Boston. Growing up, I was fortunate to have a supportive family and many opportunities to develop myself through dance and skating lessons, as well as the activities of our Lutheran church, located just two doors down the road. From an early age, religion and spirituality interested me. I attended Lutheran summer camp and Sunday School, and became active in the youth group. In my early years, I often felt some protective universal force that seemed to manifest just when I was headed for trouble. On the other hand, I struggled with the concept of God, discrepancies between my ideas and understanding of the Bible at the time, and with establishing a secure place for faith in my life.

Even though I lacked discipline in my schoolwork and wasn't inclined to practice dance or music much, my parents and several teachers recognized my creative talents, some even referring to me as "gifted." But for reasons I never understood, I found it difficult to fit in and was tormented by my peers for years on end. The daily verbal assaults—in the classroom, on the school bus, while walking around town—created tremendous anxiety and self-doubt, and a feeling of having two selves: on one hand, I was this young person with a lot of potential, but then here were these other kids, convinced I was an ugly loser, a social

CLAUDIA HEIMAN, 29, A WRITER AND FILMMAKER, AND ARTS ADMINISTRATOR FOR THE COMMONWEALTH OF MASSACHUSETTS, HAS PRACTICED NICHIREN DAISHONIN'S BUDDHISM WITH THE SOKA GAKKAI INTERNATIONAL (SGI) FOR NEARLY SEVEN YEARS.

liability, someone not worth getting to know. Kids I did befriend usually pretended not to like me when others were around, and some ditched me altogether over time. Books, music, imagination, and my cat Rufus provided consistency and escape. Only years later would I realize how much my inner life was shaped by the terror at school and the intense loneliness.

When the opportunity arose to spend my sophomore year in high school with a host family in Santiago, Chile, with the American Field Service Program, I jumped at the chance to shake things up. It was an incredibly difficult but ultimately successful year of immersion, from which I emerged fluent in Spanish and buoyant with a connection to my host culture. I returned, however, with ambivalence toward the U.S. and my life at home, and a raging identity crisis. In an attempt to figure who I was and where exactly I belonged in the world, I applied to college in Canada and spent two years in a cinema studies program. During my freshman year, I began experiencing severe depression and anxiety at crucial deadlines and exam-time, when it was essential that I succeed. Physically and mentally overwhelmed, I again sought out the church, but apart from enjoying the hymns, I didn't connect or find comfort in its members or activities. New Age books provided superficial relief for a while, but repeating affirmations soon fell flat. I began to worry obsessively about everything and withdraw from other people. Physically, I broke down, caught every cold

Books, music, imagination, and my cat Rufus provided consistency and escape.

and flu that blew in, and found myself wandering around campus alone, overcaffeinated and exhausted. At the close of my sophomore year, I decided to focus my studies more intensely on film production and transferred to art school in Boston. One year later, I transferred again to Northeastern University to study English.

While on a semester abroad in London during my senior year at Northeastern, this constant upheaval caught up with me: I hit rock bottom and felt suicidal. In retrospect, this painful situation was a great benefit in my life, as it marked a turning point: I now knew I needed a spiritual foundation, although I wasn't yet sure in what form. Shortly after returning to Boston, a friend saw how much I was suffering and shared with me her Buddhist practice, which had deeply changed her life. She invited two other women who were Buddhists over to her house, where we chanted *Nam-myoho-renge-kyo* ("devotion to the mystic law of cause and effect in the universe through sound and teaching") in front of her altar and talked about how Buddhism views human suffering. I was immediately struck by the sound of the chanting, which instead of being atonal and funereal, was quick, light, and harmonious. The chanting lifted my spirits and left a deep impression, as did the people I met. These Buddhists were cheerful, bright, and straightforward—and, contrary to my expectations, from very diverse backgrounds: the suburbs, the inner city, and a range of countries, including Japan, Jamaica, Korea, and Germany. People shared their own experiences with Buddhism and assured me that if I continued to chant, I would not only be able to overcome depression, but I could develop compassion, wisdom, and courage to bring out my highest potential.

> Buddhism gave me a a larger spiritual framework in which to work through my suffering.

The practice and core concepts of Buddhism made sense to me. It felt like I had always known how to chant; that I'd come home. There was something very powerful and life-affirming about the belief in the absolute sanctity of all life and the interconnectedness of all things, and the potential for every human being to transform a life of suffering into one of happiness and greater value. This gave me hope. I had already seen a dramatic change in my friend, Julia, who seemed so confident, settled, and fulfilled. Needless to say, I considered this practice of chanting *Nam-myoho-renge-kyo* twice a day to be worth a try!

Almost immediately, things began to shift in a more positive direction. Buddhism gave me a practical daily structure and a larger spiritual framework in which to work through my suffering. I had a daily "place" to go to which, for the first time, didn't involve fleeing to another college or country. The more I allowed myself to relax into the rhythmical chant-ing, the more I felt a connection with the ebb and flow of the universe, and with a more calm, and happy life state. For hours and then days at a time I felt more energetic, self-aware, and appreciative of my life and the people in it—a warmth like the sun, after emerging from behind clouds. As I applied myself to my practice and study, I was inspired by the following passage from Nichiren, the thirteenth-century founder of this sect of Buddhism:

> When deluded, one is called an ordinary being, but when enlight-ened, one is called a Buddha. This is similar to a tarnished mirror that will shine like a jewel when polished. A mind now clouded by the illusions of the innate darkness of life is like a tarnished mirror, but when polished, it is sure to become like a clear mirror, reflect-ing the essential nature of phenomena and the true aspect of reality.
>
> Nichiren, *On Attaining Buddhahood in This Lifetime*, 1255

I kept polishing and polishing myself, morning and evening—even on those mornings when I didn't want to get out of bed and go to class. Despite my own laziness at times, I noticed a direct correlation between my practice of chanting and my daily life: when I made the time to chant, all the day's details would somehow fall into place. With some small suc-cesses under my belt, plus deepened discipline and vigor from daily chanting, I began to feel the clarity and confidence I needed to finish the things I had started, including my schoolwork. I felt lighter in spirit and more able to connect with friends and colleagues. I began to enjoy creative writing again and even served as co-editor of the Northeastern literary magazine. A consistent practice of chanting, taking action, and chanting again was unlike any earlier "attempt to cope": my life was actu-ally changing. At the end of a difficult semester, I finally received my

B.A. in English and graduated first in my class—after five years of study in four universities in three countries. This was a tremendous personal accomplishment, one that exceeded my own expectations as a student and as a human being. I knew that chanting was at the root of my having pulled myself together after so many years of struggle. Determined to continue to change and develop my life, I made a lifelong commitment to Buddhism in September of 1994, six months after first chanting *Nam-myoho-renge-kyo*.

I can look back now over the last seven years and see that my health has improved to the point where I only catch the occasional cold, and I don't fall back into my old emotional pit. The self-slandering has nearly disappeared as I've come to recognize my own strength and feel joy at just being alive. Having overcome so much, I can break the shell of my lesser self and encourage others to just press on and not give up. My life has expanded to a wide circle of friends and family including a wonderful man, John—a musician, fellow Buddhist, and my fiancé—and a successful career in arts administration. I am steadily developing as a writer and filmmaker, and look forward to bringing more of my ideas and life experiences to light.

> Naturally, problems and obstacles still arise, but my heart is full of hope.

I've also become very active in the Soka Gakkai International movement for peace, culture, and education, taking responsibility to support other young people and host events at our beautiful New England Culture Center. Naturally, problems and obstacles still arise—being human, it's impossible to avoid them—but I don't feel so swayed by external circumstances because I have a solid Buddhist practice and my heart is full of hope.

To close, I'd like to include a quote from SGI President Daisaku Ikeda: "A great human revolution in just a single individual will help achieve a change in the destiny of a nation and further, a change in the destiny of all humankind." This has been my experience. Many thanks for the opportunity to share it.

I'M A MUTT

Hanuman Goleman

IN FIFTH GRADE I was asked what my religion was. It was then that I first thought about my religious identity and decided I am a "Bu-Hin-Chris-Jew." My father, born Jewish, met my mother, born Christian, at a Buddhist meditation course. They were married by their Hindu guru. Therefore, "Bu-Hin-Chris-Jew" makes perfect sense to me. I am a mongrel of religious and spiritual lineages, a product of religious diversity. In my family all the sources of our spiritual background are respected. We celebrate the spirit of each tradition. These rituals are a time to get together and be joyous, whether lighting Hanukkah candles or gathering with friends at a *Bhandara*, the feast held on the anniversary of the Guru's passing away.

My father grew up celebrating holidays in a reform Jewish household. My grandmother has told me that my father's birth was part of a conscious effort to increase the Jewish population of the world after it was decimated in WWII. Whether I am considered Jewish depends on to whom I'm talking; traditionally, one is Jewish only if one's mother is Jewish. I am simply happy to respect a tradition that has shaped me. Regardless of whether others consider me Jewish or not, I feel it is part of my identity. I have looked forward to Passover through the years as a jovial family

> I am a mongrel of religious and spiritual lineages.

HANUMAN GOLEMAN, 24, RECENTLY GRADUATED FROM ANTIOCH COLLEGE AND NOW LIVES, PLAYS, AND WORKS IN OAKLAND, CALIFORNIA.

time. It gives me a sense of connectedness with my family's past, and the tribulations and triumphs of my ancestors.

My mother was born in England into a nonpracticing Anglican family. It was American culture, however, that exposed me to Christianity: during December it's nearly impossible to escape Christmas. My first theatrical role was even Christian in its content—I was a shepherd boy in the local Catholic church's Christmas pageant. Although we never went to church or temple, during the holiday season our house was a mix of menorahs (the Hanukkah candle-holders) and pine trees. My practice of Christianity is limited to a few holidays, but I'm perfectly willing to believe that Jesus Christ was a fully realized being.

My parents were both drawn to India in their twenties. My father found himself there during his doctoral research on states of mind, and my mother found herself there after traveling overland on her own from Europe. My father had been spending time with Neem Karoli Baba, a Hindu yogi, and he invited my mother to come back with him to meet the Baba. Within a few months, Neem Karoli Baba, otherwise known as Maharaj-ji, presided over my parents' wedding. Their experience with this man affected their lives so deeply that, for the next few years, devotion to him was a large component of their daily practice, and their social circle revolved around him. This is the time that I was born. We lived in a communal house in Queens that was full of Maharaj-ji devotees. Every week the house was packed with meditation classes and people gathering for *kirtan*, devotional chanting. I have vague memories of being lulled to sleep by *Sri Ram Jai Ram* as it wafted out of the windows to Queens Boulevard. To this day the people from that house are all like my aunts and uncles. Wherever I go in the country it seems that one of them is not far away, always willing to help me if I need it.

This brings us to the "Bu" in "Bu-Hin-Chris-Jew." I am most drawn

I have vague memories of being lulled to sleep by "sri ram jai ram" as it wafted out of the windows to Queens Boulevard.

toward Buddhism for my own spiritual work. Although I believe that ultimately all religions pursue similar spiritual goals, I like Buddhism because of its direct, honest, and no-nonsense approach. I did my first meditation retreat in 1991 when I was fifteen years old. It was a young-adult retreat at Insight Meditation Society in Barre, Massachusetts, taught by U Pandita, a Burmese monk. Although I didn't take it very seriously—and it was nowhere near as strict or strenuous as an adult retreat—it must have planted some seeds because I was back for more in '94. This time it was an adult retreat, and I practiced with even more sincerity and discipline. I was moved deeply by my experiences there and have tried to do one retreat a year since then. In the fall of 1997 I spent a semester in Bodh Gaya, where the historical Buddha sat beneath the Bodhi Tree. I was a part of the Antioch Buddhist Studies program. It was there that I studied Buddhist philosophy in-depth. The regularity of my daily practice varies, but I nevertheless feel a long-term commitment.

"The mind is a belligerent puppy— easy to train, difficult to discipline."

Buddhism has informed all aspects of my life. As a musician I find that many of the lyrics I write are influenced by Buddhism. For example, I wrote a tune called "Everyone you know is gonna die someday" as a reflection on the First Noble Truth. My interests in school have also been guided largely by insights and understanding that I owe to Buddhist practice. In college, my major was a combination of theater and cognitive psychology. Buddhism informed my cognitive psych interests by directing me toward discussions of mental constructs and "memes" (self-replicating ideas). My senior performance, called "The Mind Is a Belligerent Puppy—Easy to Train, Difficult to Discipline," was a series of pieces that I wrote expressing Buddhist ideas in the guise of cognitive psychology. One act was based on the idea that identifying with our thoughts becomes a prison for us, and the realization, "I am not this thought," can open the door to severing those attachments. In another act, a slick con-artist type represents mental functions, like labeling and selective memory. Illustrating how those habits dictate our reality, he assures us that everything is just fine the way it is and encourages the audience not to trouble our little heads about it. He concludes with, "Sometimes I just sit back and thank one of my best works, God, for TV. The more mindless, the more better. Keeping 'em thinking they're thinking, ya know?"

Even though my main practice is Buddhist, I accept many religious truths rather than thinking that God is any one thing. Reflecting on the characteristics of infiniteness and everything-ness that are attributed to God, I could never understand the arguments between the various religions, each saying that its God is the true God. To me that is perfectly reasonable, but just because one person is right doesn't mean that everyone else is wrong. It seems to me that if there is only one God and that God is everything, then everyone must be right. With all the different languages and cultural realities, it makes all the sense in the world that God would have thousands of names and be recognized by varying aspects.

> AS I see it, all things are of divinity —even small things like cracks in the sidewalk.

As I see it, all things are of divinity—even small things like cracks in the sidewalk. It is only our mental and emotional patterning that keeps us from noticing the divinity as it is taking place right in front of us all the time. Our attention is caught up in habits. Buddhism is about being aware: simply seeing that patterning and not catering to it. It is shining light through the thick fog of those mental and emotional patterns. In being aware we see the divine nature of all things, and so we come closer to the state of divinity that is all around. On the contrary to being at odds with other religions, I think that uncovering unhealthy patterns in ourselves, as is taught in Buddhism, is beneficial to the practice of any religion.

LIFE AS A VIETNAMESE NUN

Sister Kristine (Thich Nu Pho-Chau)

MANY PEOPLE, particularly the Vietnamese elders in my community, ask me why I have chosen to be a Buddhist nun. After all, they say, you are a young woman living in America, with a lot of opportunities for your future—why, of all possible choices, would you choose the monastic path? They think of America as a wealthy country in which I can fulfill any material desire. Compared to poor countries such as Vietnam, America is like heaven. So my elders wonder why I trade what they've always wanted—a good life—for the strict discipline of the monastery right here in America. In addition, they have a stereotype that those who choose a monastic life do so because they are poor, lovesick, want to run away from government duty, or because they hate their life.

For me, it is different. I'm not poor, lovesick, or hating life in this world—but I also don't want to have a life centered on getting a good house and car, providing for a family, fulfilling my desires at the mall. I want a life that is meaningful. To me, what is meaningful is to have peace and tranquility every day so that I can dedicate my energy to helping the people around me. I don't want to work hard in a big company just to chase after impermanent pleasures, because at the end of my life, I won't be able to bring the house, car, money, prestige, or anything else with me.

SISTER KRISTINE (THICH NU PHO-CHAU), 25, A GRADUATE OF UNIVERSITY OF HAWAII–MANOA IN BIOLOGY, IS NOW IN THE THIRD YEAR OF THE MONASTIC TRAINING PROGRAM AT HAYWARD BUDDHIST CENTER, CALIFORNIA, AND WAS RECENTLY ORDAINED AS A SHRAMANERIKA IN THE MAHAYANA TRADITION.

But honestly, it's not always easy to inspire myself in the path I've chosen, which is stripped-down of normal pleasures. So when my *bodhichitta* fades, I remember the words of my teacher, who asks me, "Do you want to live a life tied down to two kids and a husband, surrounded by the four walls of a small house?" My answer is no. I want to have freedom, freedom from the barriers of a spouse and children, and freedom to expand my heart out for everyone, not just my close family and friends.

> I don't want to have a life centered on fulfilling my desires at the mall.

I began thinking about becoming a Buddhist nun when I was in the ninth grade. I asked my parents for permission to live in the monastery, but they said no. Being the oldest daughter of eight children made it very tough for me to get my parents' approval. Asian parents usually depend a lot on their daughters, especially the oldest. I had many responsibilities, including going to every doctor's appointment to translate for my parents and siblings, since my parents could not speak English. I also had chores—cooking, babysitting, and helping my siblings with their homework.

For eight years, I held on to my dream of being a nun. I wasn't able to begin making this dream come true until I graduated from college. Upon graduating, I realized I was at the juncture where I could choose the course of the rest of my life. I strengthened my resolve to be a monastic and then set about searching for a suitable sangha and teacher for my Buddhist studies. My parents' approval was still an issue, so I waited until after I was accepted in the sangha to tell them that I was going to live in the monastery and become a nun. They were very sad and disappointed. My mother cried because she said she felt like she was losing her daughter to another family. They tried to talk me out of it by saying that California was not a good place to live because it had earthquakes, that monastic life was too rigorous, and that monastic discipline would be a hardship for the rest of my life.

I was finally able to persuade them to give me permission to join the sangha and even to support me. Once in a while, my father asks me to come home; this request makes me sad and angry at the same time because it seems like my parents don't support my chosen path the way the parents of my dharma brothers and sisters do. However, when I look more deeply, I am thankful that my parents are so strict with me because it makes my bodhichitta stronger. Their questioning the seriousness of my decision helps me feel even more determined in my monastic path. I think also they were concerned I would back out of my decision later in life. In my tradition, returning to lay life would bring shame upon my family. At the same time, it is considered an honor to the family and community when one chooses to join the monastic sangha. So, these days, even though my parents don't say so directly, deep down I know they are proud of me.

Despite the fact that they were reluctant at the beginning about my becoming a nun, my family now supports me both spiritually and materially. My parents and younger sister flew from Virginia to California to attend my *shramanerika* ordination on July 21, 2000. Their presence meant a lot to me. The lay community also supports me a great deal by making donations of vegetables, rice, clothing, and money to the monastery. Once, when they came and saw my face was pale, they became concerned about my health. They asked whether I needed to take vitamins, because they would buy and donate them to me. I owe my life to the Triple Gem, the lay community, and to my parents because all that I have comes from and belongs to them. The bed I sleep in, the clothes I wear, the food I eat, even the computer I am now using—all of these are not mine.

My training does not allow me to take these gifts for granted. There is a verse in Vietnamese that says:

Even though my parents don't say so directly, deep down I know they are proud of me.

A rice-grain from the donor
As heavy as Mountain Tu Di

Eat but do not practice mindfully
Wear fur and horn to repay.

What this verse means is that even one grain of rice is a precious gift
that I must eat with mindfulness and gratitude. If I don't, if I become lazy
about my Buddhist practice, then I'll be reborn as an animal in the next
life, furry, with a horn rather than a mouth, to repay what I didn't express
in gratitude as a human.

My life at the monastery is very
regulated, and almost everything
is done as a group, with other
monastics. Our sangha wakes up
at 5:30 in the morning and begins
the day with chanting and meditation. After breakfast we have

*Even one grain of rice
is a precious gift that I must eat
with mindfulness and gratitude.*

classes on dharma three days of the week, taught by my teacher and other
teachers from nearby pagodas. The other weekdays I spend this time
studying, memorizing sutras, and doing clerical work for the monastery
administration. Lunch is followed by a period of mindful working meditation, doing such tasks as cleaning and sweeping, gardening, or folding
letters. At 7:00 in the evening, we chant and meditate again.

Becoming an official member of the Hayward Buddhist Center
requires a six-month stay in the monastery. During those six months,
the teacher carefully scrutinized my every action: eating, walking, talking, studying, and associating with others. He then determined whether
I had the capacity and ability to become a nun. After the Taking of Vows
Ceremony, which is when my hair got shaven off, I began studying Buddhism formally. I had to live in the monastery as a novice for two more
years before I could be ordained with the Ten Precepts to be a shramanerika.

Within the next four years, I will have my full ordination to become a
bhikshuni, and my training will be completed. The full ordination is
equivalent to getting a bachelor's degree at the university level. I have not
yet decided what to do after my full ordination. I can either stay where

I am now or go into the world to help and serve people. Whatever I do, I wish to bring happiness and peace of mind to everyone around me and then reward this merit to my parents and all sentient beings. For the next life, I wish to continue being a nun or monk, but I pray to enter the monastic life early in childhood and follow the bodhisattva's vows.

My life as a monastic here in America is a little different than how it would be in Vietnam. Although I only lived in Vietnam for eight years in my childhood, I have heard quite a bit about the monastic life in Vietnam. Vietnamese monastics start their day a bit earlier, beginning the morning chant around 4:00 or 5:00. Another difference is that the nuns in Vietnam spend more of their time doing labor, such as planting vegetables and making incense to sell to lay people at the open market to support their monastic lives. When comparing the monastic life in America and Vietnam, I feel even more blessed because the lay people provide everything we need, whereas in Vietnam, the nuns have to work more since the lay practitioners are too poor to provide all material supports. They have fewer conveniences, so they work more and have less time for studying. But just because we nuns here have more time doesn't mean we are any brighter. Sometimes I think the Vietnamese nuns are more studious because they don't take their time for granted and therefore use their time more efficiently.

I enjoy living in the monastery very much. I feel that I have finally found my real home. When I compare my life to those of my peers, I feel

I also don't have to worry about having "a bad hair day"—I don't have any hair.

grateful for the monastic life. By living in the monastery, I am able to avoid grasping at material gratification and thereby creating more bad karma. My personal life is very simplified. I no longer have to worry what to wear tomorrow because I know exactly what I will wear—a gray uniform! I have three pairs of exactly the same outfit to choose from. The daily clothing for monastics at our pagoda is very simple and easy to distinguish: gray uniforms for the novices and brown for the fully ordained. Having such a simple outfit helps me to focus on studying, rather than on my clothes. The robes themselves are simple and cheap, but acquiring them is anything but simple—not just anyone can wear them. One of our new American sangha members asked me where she could buy the robes that I was wearing. I told her: "You can't buy them because no one will sell them to you. But if you ordain and become a nun, then these clothes will be given to you." She gave me a look implying "That's not fair."

> I enjoy living in the monastery very much. I feel that I have finally found my real home.

I also don't have to worry about having "a bad hair day"—I don't have any hair. Food is also no longer a big concern, although I am mindful of what and when I eat. I cannot just open the refrigerator anytime I am hungry. Instead, I only eat during community meal hours, which helps me maintain a healthy body and teaches me to control my desires for food. There is a saying for monastics: "Three less and one more." The three less are eating, wearing, and sleeping, and the one more is practicing mindfulness. Everything we do in the monastery functions to help us decrease our wants because with fewer wants, we will suffer less. Our goal is to cross the sea of suffering of birth and death, but only fewer wants and more peace of mind will bring us closer to that further seashore.

In closing, I would like to share with you one of my favorite verses:

Universal Worthy Bodhisattva's Verse of Exhortation

This day is already done
Our lives are that much less
We're like fish in a shrinking pond
What joy is there in this?
Great Assembly!
We should be diligent and vigorour

As if our own heads were at stake
Only be mindful of impermanence
And be careful not to be lax.

DRUGS AND THE DHARMA

Kenneth Lee

IT MIGHT SEEM STRANGE to associate drug use with Buddhist practice when Buddhist precepts specifically prohibit intoxicants that alter consciousness. Yet, during the '60s quite a few American Buddhists saw drugs as a method for expanding their own minds in search of a spiritual state. Even today there are some of us on the American Buddhist periphery who have attempted to perform our own internal alchemy in the name of the Dharma. My own experiments began in high school, at a time when I saw Buddhism as a way to take control of my own mind and to map my internal landscape. I had learned in Zen that "to see one's true nature is to become Buddha." I was eager to see my own true nature, but there seemed to be no agreement about an expedient way to get there. I was getting impatient with traditional forms of practice; they seemed backward and archaic. I had heard that psychedelics could expand the mind. After a thorough reading of the '50s beat writers, like Jack Kerouac and Gary Snyder, I decided while in my junior year of high school to attempt the path of drugs outlined in the work of these authors.

After a thorough reading of the '50s Beat writers, I decided to attempt the path of drugs outlined in the work of these authors.

KENNETH LEE, 23, IS WRITING UNDER A DIFFERENT NAME.

I proceeded methodically, like a scientist, though I was both the observer and the observed. I took copious notes on my experiments, in which I sat in full-lotus position with all my attention focused inward as the drugs took effect. I have to admit there was some degree of recreation, like I was a kid with a new chemistry set trying to make things blow up just because I could. But overall I was very serious about examining my own brain in its state of chemically induced dysfunction. So I used comparably safe substances like LSD, 'shrooms, and amphetamines. These tools did in fact help me break my mind down into pieces that I could examine, disassemble, and reassemble in new ways. The drugs helped me to lose control of my everyday mental processes so that I could see into the depths of my unconscious and shatter the fragile framework of consistent reality. For example, I remember on one occasion I stopped perceiving the continuity of time. Instead of the one smooth, continuous moment that we normally experience, I perceived things as a discontinuous series of unconnected instants slamming into each other, like falling dominos. Through the trial of these chemicals I discovered firsthand that the mind is a shifting world, an alterable climate not fully under my control.

Although these were dangerous experiments, psychologically, if not always physically, they enabled me to confront the complex specters and memories that haunted the corridors of my mind. And as I wandered further and further into this world, I was always a little afraid that I would become lost in these halls and never truly return, and that almost happened in what was a final experiment in my drug career with LSD.

I had used LSD before, and my thorough reading of medical journals seemed to indicate that its physiological effects were negligible. However, I had never "tripped" for more than a brief period before, hours at a time but never more than that. This time, I decided to create a period of hallucination lasting several days. I truly wanted to push myself to my limits, to find out what would happen to my mind when it stopped having something to hold onto. In earlier experiments, I always felt an awareness that however strange, if I waited it out, things would return to normal. This time I wanted to extend the experiment so long that I would forget what normal was. In essence I wanted to "open wide the doors of perception… through a prolonged derangement of the senses," to borrow the words of Aldous Huxley.

At first, I saw all the things I'd seen before, such as "tracers"—ghostly motion trails and curving space. I felt my ability to connect with time slip, and I had feelings of sudden euphoria and sadness. All of this I was prepared for. However, at some point I completely lost my grip of reality. I forgot who I was. I reached some kind of vision of no-self, in which, paradoxically, my absence was manifestly apparent. I was experiencing something I had never felt before: instead of the normal chatter in my mind, there was only a hallway empty of human life. If there was a Ken, I had forgotten that he had ever existed. To the degree in which he was noticed, all that was left was a hole implying that something was missing. This absence didn't bother me, in

BUT I was not prepared for the moment when my mind stopped playing around altogether and turned on me.

part because it felt as though there was no one to be bothered. I was totally unaware of my body or of any personal sensations; all that remained was the sense of the hallway existing on its own.

Unfortunately, things started to go very wrong. A mild nausea, probably caused by the long period of fasting, brought me back to my body. However something was missing. I didn't know who I was, and I certainly didn't know that I was on LSD. I began to panic. None of my previous training had made me ready for this. I had been playing games with my mind, and they had prepared me for some vicissitudes, some twists, and some bucking. But I was not prepared for the moment when my mind stopped playing around altogether and turned on me. It was like the difference of being in a nightmare when you're aware that it's a nightmare versus when you believe fully that something terrible is happening to you. The level of confusion and fear existed at a completely different level of intensity.

He said my eyes looked like an animal's, with strange dilated pupils, and he could tell that I was very, very frightened.

I was just trying to fumble into lotus position when suddenly the idea came to my brain that I was having a heart attack. I was scared, alone, and confused to the point of near noncomprehension. But I had enough awareness to know that whoever I was, there was something terribly wrong with my thoughts. It scared me tremendously. How could I tell what was hallucination and what portended imminent death when I knew that something was wrong with the basic functioning of my mind?

I stumbled into my younger brother's room out of some kind of homing instinct. He was half asleep with the light from the hallway falling on his face. I knew he was familiar to me, but I didn't recognize him, and he could tell. Later he told me that this really scared him. He said my eyes looked like an animal's, with strange dilated pupils, and he could tell that I was very, very frightened. I don't remember what I said, but I think I used the words *stroke* and *help*.

Knowing of my experiment, he quickly ascertained that I was not in fact dying but in the midst of a "bad trip." He tried to calm me down, but every few seconds I'd forget who and where I was and would start to panic. My brother fetched my cousin and between them they sat a bodhisattva-like vigil, reminding me who and where I was every few minutes. For hours the dialogue went like this:

Me: "Who am I?"

Brother: "You are Kenneth Jacob Lee."

Me: "Kenneth Jacob Lee…. Who am I?"

Cousin: "You are Kenneth Jacob Lee."

No matter how much I concentrated, I couldn't hold on to that information because it seemed somehow artificial. I couldn't connect to my long-term memory—the past was a gaping mouth trying to devour the present and digest it into invisibility. I couldn't remember anything, or even begin to understand anything without it being devoured.

I knew that my mind was damaged, but I couldn't keep track of who I was or what was going on. It was the most frightened I've ever been in my life. Perhaps my attachment to self was so strong that suddenly being without a self put me in a continual state of panic. I was not comfortable with this form of no-self; I yearned for the narration that provided me with an identity and a context for all my actions. At one point my cousin attempted a Zen shout, which liberated my fragile eggshell sense of identity for a fleeting moment before it was smashed again by the mental onslaught.

Eventually, just as the sun was starting to come up, my brother and cousin managed to get me to sit in lotus position. Combined with the posture and the slow, even breathing, I calmed down and lost the sense of panic. Still, the effects of the chemical took another hour or two to fade to a level in which I could remember who and where I was. As soon as I realized that I was on LSD, control came back and I was in the clear for the rest of the ride, enjoying my own internal terrain.

This was the last experiment I attempted, not because it was a bad trip but because I realized that my methodology was seriously flawed. First, my vision of no-self was, in retrospect, not the kind of no-self one experiences through Buddhist practice. The masters say that when one has a true sense of no-self, one is essentially connected to all beings. The vision of no-self I had was just the opposite: no connection to anything whatsoever, not even the fluidity of my own experience in the real world. Second, for the whole time that I was mixing chemicals and my brain, I

The vision of no-self I had was just the opposite: no connection to anything whatsoever, not even the fluidity of my own experience in the real world.

thought I was really exploring my mind. In fact, my practice had no foundation: I didn't *really* understand the way my mind worked normally, much less when it was twisted out of shape. Third, I realized that in a certain sense my study had been based upon an artificial vision of "objectivity." Although grounded in experience, I had imagined myself as somehow separate from my own mind, able to observe things without being affected by them. The whole time I had been taking notes and abstracting. Not only was I removing myself one more step from reality with drugs, I even removed myself from that reality with my imagined vision of objectivity. I was essentially moving *further* from my own reality, from my buddha nature, not closer. Even though I learned much from my experiments about my strengths and weaknesses, it's clear to me now that the best technique for me to explore my own mind is not this internal alchemy, but mindful awareness beginning in meditation and then extended into the action of daily life.

Getting Off the Cushion

Jonathan Drummey

I GRADUATED FROM COLLEGE with a degree in playwrighting, a lot of anxiety about what to do next, and a deep fear of how bad life would be if I weren't in grad school or didn't have a good job. So I went to work as a technical writer for software development companies, figuring that would pay the bills while I did more creative work in my off-hours. I thought it would be a temporary measure while gathering experience and resources to do what I really wanted—whatever that was.

Work became the top priority so I wouldn't starve, and I didn't write more plays. Instead I became absorbed in the challenges of my job. Over the next several years I picked up more and different responsibilities, traveled the world, worked with clients on exciting new products and services, and had tremendous career success by any typical measure. Friends and family only saw me every few weeks and often less, and romantic relationships never had a chance because they always came in second. Eventually I lost count of the number of gatherings I'd declined, missed, or skipped due to the need to spend a few more hours at work and complete just one more task. The "Hi, I didn't know you were in the country!" greetings went from being amusing to tiring, and I started wondering what life was like for people who were able to get together on Sunday for swimming or on Wednesday to watch a favorite TV show.

Then, for the first time in my professional life, one morning I woke up not wanting to go in to the office anymore. I questioned why I was work-

JONATHAN DRUMMEY, 30, AFTER WRAPPING UP A SABBATICAL, HAS BEGUN WORK IN A NONPROFIT TO SUPPORT GRASSROOTS PATRONAGE OF THE CREATIVE LIFE.

ing so hard, and for what, and what I was doing with my life. Instead of viewing the state of my life as "I'll be happy later when…" I asked myself, "Why am I not happy now?" I looked at other career options and tried one, but varying what I did for forty or fifty-plus hours per week just wasn't enough. I began to pay attention to my well-being in other ways: spending more time outdoors, changing my eating habits, reading more, and learning meditation.

The books I read included volumes of philosophy and Eastern thought such as the *Tao Te Ching* by Lao Tzu, Thich Nhat Hanh's *The Miracle of Mindfulness*, and Tsai Chih Chung's *Zen Speaks*. I'd read some of these when I was younger and had retreated from the Buddhist notion of emptiness, misunderstanding it as nihilism and being afraid of that nothingness. This time, I understood emptiness as like an empty flowerpot, the space in which things grow. That stumbling block gone, the other insights I was having felt intuitively right. I understood that I'd gone into playwrighting as a way of teaching others and had fallen out of it because I had no wisdom to share. So I desired to learn more, about myself and about the world around me, so I could one day be a teacher.

Instead of viewing the state of my life as "I'll be happy later when…" I asked myself, "why am I not happy now?"

In meditation I found quiet attention to the present moment instructive and exhilarating. My increasing awareness helped me break some bad habits and notice others. Perhaps the best example for me is the walk home from the subway. I used to charge home, moving quickly and practically running up the stairs so I could get inside to do something else. Now—when I remember to—I walk, and breathe, and can't help but smile at the very ordinary sights that become special when I'm not worrying about the seven things I've got to get done after lunch.

I saw changes elsewhere as well. My relationships used to follow a certain trajectory, one that started in happy-go-lucky bliss and ended with a slow, stagnant flicker that eventually, agonizingly went out. I was hardly ever sure of what I wanted and hesitant to commit for fear of getting what I didn't want—but I wasn't much sure of what that was either. It was only a couple of years ago that I finally realized that I was causing the stagnation by not opening myself up to my partners. Even through the upheavals in my work life, as I opened up, my interactions with friends and family were especially satisfying, and they grew even better as I decided to take some time off and make my relationship with Katherine, my current girlfriend, more of a priority.

But in each attempt the relationship would build to a certain point and die.

Romantically, Katherine and I were doing the best we ever had on our third try at a relationship. She is a passionate person, a born leader who makes people feel more alive just by being in her presence. She places tremendous hopes and dreams on having a lifelong mate, desiring to have a profound influence on just one other person in her life even as she often misses the influence she has on many others. Perhaps her greatest challenge is that when a significant relationship fails, the end of the dream fills her with self-doubt and recrimination. In me, Katherine found an emotional innocence that sometimes led to deep sharing and sometimes to pain when I was being infuriatingly oblivious. We agreed that my abilities at logical analysis complemented her passion and emotion.

The attraction between us had always been such that even when apart in a crowded room we would gravitate toward one another and pick up the conversation of our lives from wherever it had left off. Every couple of years we would wonder why we weren't together and start things up again, each of us with the small "Maybe this time it lasts?" voice in our heads. But in each attempt the relationship would build to a certain point—different each time around—and die.

We thought this third time around would be different because of changes we'd each been making in our lives. Katherine was seeking a better balance between her hopes and the misery they caused when they weren't fulfilled. I was becoming more self-aware, better at communicating what was happening with me, and easing into practice of the Five Precepts. She supported my meditation practice, I supported her spiritual practice, and we both enjoyed the changes in each other.

When we started this latest incarnation of our relationship, we had mutually agreed-upon, minimal expectations of what would happen between us; a bond that was stronger than friendship, but less than a committed relationship. As the months passed our feelings changed and grew stronger, and we took tentative steps forward. In our past attempts Katherine had pushed to deepen the relationship and I'd resisted; this time around I was the one who was initially more open to moving ahead and expressing the love I felt. We decided to get together one night to talk about what that meant, what our plans were, and what commitments we might make. I was a bit nervous, but I thought the attitude of openness and honesty that we both shared would lead us to something more than we'd had before.

As we talked, we were both truthful and honest—sometimes brutally so, but neither of us was really listening.

That night in Katherine's living room, I decided the conversation should begin with what was happening for each of us, so we could have a solid understanding of one another before we got into where we were going. I started by telling her some things I'd learned from delving into my psyche, then my plans for the future. I intended to visit family and friends around New England, to spend the fall riding my motorcycle around the country, to continue my meditation practice, and to go on a couple of retreats. As I shared my plans and myself, all I noticed was that Katherine was very quiet throughout the hour or so I talked.

She said when I was finished, "In all that, you didn't mention me once. I thought we were talking about the future of us."

"I just wanted to let you know what was going on with me," I replied. That was true, and I knew she was also speaking the truth and had identified something deeper. I felt I'd tripped over my self-absorption. I began looking inward, trying to discern why I was being self-centered so I could better communicate with Katherine.

"What sort of relationship do we really have?" she asked.

I took her question literally and responded with an explanation, telling her what I knew and did not know even as I tried to be aware and mindful of the roiling tension and emotions. I thought if she understood me, understood what I was saying, then from that connection we could continue the conversation and move on. However, Katherine was still caught up in her reaction, feeling she had no place in my life and that her dream had ended again. As we talked, we were both truthful and honest—sometimes brutally so, but neither of us was really listening. We never got to discuss where she was or our future together, and within a few minutes we'd become strangers to one another, both of us stunned.

We were bewildered at how quickly our relationship had moved from something wonderful to a great source of hurt and trouble. Katherine was angry with herself perhaps even more than she was upset with me, for she was feeling that same old pain again. I was in shock, feeling empathy for Katherine and pain from being rejected when I'd tried to share myself, and unable to express any of that. I could only dully respond to Katherine's feelings of loss and betrayal. Within two weeks our relationship ended. Katherine turned to others for help; I very much wanted to provide comfort but could do little for her other than reach out through mutual friends. She eventually recovered and started a new relationship, keeping a distance between us that had never existed before.

we were bewildered at how quickly our relationship had moved from something wonderful to a great source of hurt and trouble.

I had thought that with my newfound awareness our relationship would evolve and grow, but instead it took a huge step backward. I had thought I was going about the relationship in the right way, but I also knew I had done something terribly wrong. There were definite benefits to all my introspection—even in the midst of arguing with Katherine I had come to new understandings about myself—but something was missing. My practice was shaken for a while. I meditated and studied less because of doubts as to whether the path I was on was really making my life better and worries that I was doing too much navel-gazing and too little living.

With help from friends I caught a few glimmerings of understanding, but my behavior remained on my mind. Several months later, as part of the preparation for a retreat, I was asked to imagine I was going to die and to make whatever preparations and farewells were necessary. It became clear that the most important thing for me to do, more than anything else, was to fully apologize to Katherine.

I finally realized that on the night our relationship fell apart I had not opened up to Katherine at all—only to myself. It had become so important to me to understand what was going on in myself and express that understanding to Katherine that I could not respond to her with compassion. In fact, in my self-absorption I had missed that basic experience of being with her from the very beginning of our conversation. I now knew how important it was to be mindful of existing relationships, even in the midst of enlightenments. I apologized to Katherine for the harm I had caused by mistaking self-centeredness for self-awareness.

I've since learned that being mindful of others is a better way to mutual understanding than trying to push my agenda. It is now easier for me to notice the feeling that I have something to say and yet hold off so I can listen to the person I'm with. And perhaps most importantly, when I feel a defensive response forming, I try to skip it and look for a response containing compassion and love.

I felt a sense of a burden being lifted as I told Katherine I was sorry and shared this story with her. It became a peace offering as I let go of my pain. Katherine hasn't forgiven me, nor has our friendship recovered. Perhaps it will—until then, I'm able to again feel a quiet joy in her company.

A WAY OF LIFE

Liane C. Yasumoto

WHEN I WAS FOUR, I began attending Dharma School at the local Jodo Shinshu Church in San Francisco. I remember being too young to understand most of what I was taught there. One teaching I found especially mystifying was the one the reverends and my teachers recited frequently: "Buddhism is a way of life." That phrase only began to have some meaning for me when I left home for the first time, just after graduating from high school, to attend a ten-day retreat for young Buddhists in Berkeley. I was anxious about leaving the comfort and safety of the home nest, but the retreat was a foretaste of the independence I'd have to cultivate when I went off to college in San Luis Obispo in the fall. It was on this retreat that I'd begin to know that leaving home meant finding my own relationship to Buddhism as a way of life.

There were twenty of us young birds from across the country, eager yet a bit apprehensive to spread our wings, gathered in the modest but comfortable house to live and learn the dharma. We were split up into four *toban*, or service groups, and given chores of cleaning, cooking, and setting up for the three services we participated in daily. The days were packed with workshops and activities. For example, we began the week with icebreakers, such as falling backward into the arms of fellow participants to learn trust. The guest speakers, who were mostly reverends, taught us practices like Buddhist etiquette, where we learned the significance of such

LIANE C. YASUMOTO, 33, IS THE EXECUTIVE DIRECTOR OF THE CORPORATION ON DISABILITIES AND TELECOMMUNICATION (CDT), A BERKELEY BASED NONPROFIT ORGANIZATION THAT WORKS TO CHANGE THE STEREOTYPICAL IMAGES OF PEOPLE WITH DISABILITIES IN THE MEDIA.

practices as bowing in reverence before lighting incense at the altar. Learning about the symbolism of things on the altar, the fresh flowers symbolizing impermanence, and the candles symbolizing "truth" and "light," enriched my appreciation of being before the shrine. My favorite part of the retreat was traveling to Enmanji Temple in Sebastopol. A Tibetan monk led us on a walking meditation, where we practiced not making eye contact with others. I remember how difficult it was to not talk for the two hours we were meditating or eating the lunch of rice and vegetables, and even harder to not make eye contact. This practice gave us a taste of the discipline it takes to focus on meditation and be in solitude. For us chatty teenagers, this was the biggest challenge of the week!

But we were also challenged to reflect on ourselves and what Buddhism meant to us. The coordinators let us know that this retreat was not simply summer camp, but instead an educational program at a religious institution. One of the required readings was Reverend Kubose's book *Everyday Suchness*, which helped me relate Buddhism to my everyday life.

I remember how difficult it was to not talk for the two hours we were meditating.... for us chatty teenagers, this was the biggest challenge of the week!

We were also given four questions on which to "think, reflect, ponder, and struggle." We were encouraged to think of our own answers, not ones that would please our parents or counselors. The four questions were: Why do I need religion? What is the uniqueness of Buddhism, when compared to the fundamental beliefs of the Judeo-Christian religion? What is the difference between Shakyamuni Buddha and Amida Buddha, and how do they differ from the Christian God? How do I live and practice as a Jodo Shinshu Buddhist?

Looking back, those four questions and the retreat experience were pivotal in my beginning to identify with a religion and way of life that I was raised with. That Buddhist "awakening" experience will remain vivid in my mind because it was there that I learned that Buddhism was not about facts like when or where the Buddha was born. Instead, I came away from the retreat with the conclusion that it was far more important to emulate *how* the Buddha lived by practicing his teachings of wisdom and compassion as a way of life. It was also important to practice the teachings of the Golden Chain, of being kind and gentle to all living things and protecting all who are weaker than myself.

I realized that we were experiencing the Jodo Shinshu teachings while we worked and lived together those ten days. For example, by waiting in long lines to take a shower we were practicing patience, one of the Six Perfections. By vacuuming the rug and watering the plants we were practicing right effort, one part of the Eightfold Noble Path. Doing chores mindfully to help the sangha as opposed to goofing off required a positive effort. I realized that staying up late listening to a friend talk about his family problems was a form of compassion. Living these lessons rather than just talking about them strengthened me as a Buddhist.

My paralysis has brought many positive opportunities.

I left for college with a sense of understanding that Buddhism really is a way of life. Over the next two years of classes, spring breaks, and summer jobs, I learned to become more independent. Around this time I began reflecting on some of the philosophies I'd learned as a kid. I came to the conclusion that being a Jodo Shinshu Buddhist could be summarized in three words: selflessness, acceptance, and impermanence. I wasn't exactly sure how to integrate these philosophies into my daily life: little did I know that I would soon be tested to deeply wrestle with all three.

Two weeks before my twentieth birthday, I was involved in an automobile accident that left me paralyzed from the neck down. While I was lying in the Intensive Care Unit immobile, not knowing whether I would ever be able to walk again, let alone move my arms, hands, or fingers, I remember feeling grateful to be alive, grateful to have a working heart and mind. Adjusting to my new situation was a challenge, but one that I embraced with my entire being. Accepting that this change was a simple fact of life enabled me to see that all aspects of life are impermanent, most especially one's physical being. At a time when I was just getting used to being on my own, I was forced into complete dependence on others. In a split second, I went from being independent to requiring attendants to assist with me with all activities of daily living—bathing, dressing, exercising, cooking, even eating. I reflected on acceptance.

The years, months, weeks, minutes, seconds, and moments that followed have not been easy. My dark days, however, have had more to do with the frustration I feel when my health isn't up to par (keeping me from keeping up with my commitments), than from dwelling on all the physical activities I can no longer do. Surprising to most people, I never went through the customary periods of bitter denial, anger, depression, or regret. My adjustment was natural and immediate. I attribute this smooth transition to a combination of forces: my family and friends' unconditional love and support gave me strength emotionally, and the teachings of the Buddha sustained me spiritually. These days, Buddhism as a way of life has taken on even richer meanings.

> The impermanence in my life has broadened my horizons and brought me great joy.

I appreciate my life as it is, realizing that my paralysis has brought many positive opportunities that I may not have ever encountered had I not become disabled. For example, I wouldn't have lived in the dorm if I hadn't become disabled, and I would've missed out on the experience of interacting with numerous people. I've also met people from all over the world because I have worked with personal assistants from various countries—Nigeria, Brazil, Nicaragua, Japan, Venezuela, Bulgaria, Indonesia, Poland, Guatemala, Switzerland, and Mongolia. These women who have worked as my personal assistants—dressing, bathing, and cooking for me—have taught me about their countries and have exposed me to their diverse communities, foods, languages, governments, and cultures.

Looking back on my thirty-three years of life, I appreciate my parents taking me to Dharma School as a child. I never realized the impact that hearing the dharma talks would have on a person. It felt like I was not ever really listening to any of the weekly sermons, but I now realize the importance of being exposed to or simply hearing the teachings, though not always able to fully grasp them. I believe that listening and practicing the dharma daily enables people to learn and grow and accumulate a reserve of practical beliefs to draw upon in times of crisis. In my case, my reserve kicked in thirteen years ago when I became disabled, and I continue to look to the wisdom of compassion of Jodo Shinshu Buddhism to guide me on my path.

GOING FOR THE GURU

Julia Hengst

A GOOD TEACHER is like a clear and truthful magic mirror; you can ask to be shown how you appear in your fullest spiritual dimension, and the teacher will find a skillful way to show you this. Then you look into the mirror of words, actions, example, and advice, given by your teacher. Once you see clearly, change is possible.

But the whole idea of "looking for a teacher," of finding a guide for a spiritual journey, was unsettling and uncomfortable for me. In the West, it's okay to rely upon science teachers to boost our SATs; it's acceptable, even expected, to have a qualified coach in sports; it's considered prudent to have an advisor on the stock market—but a spiritual teacher? Mention that and words like "cult" and "brainwashing" easily arise. While I am used to searching for the teacher, the coach, the advisor, the mentor, the counselor, and the friend, how do I recognize the person who will help me rid my mind of delusions and open my heart fully? Where is the *Lonely Planet* guidebook for that trip?

Stories about teachers can range from the magical ("He made these pills appear in his hands out of nothing, and I took them and felt so amazing!") to the mystical ("I had a vision and heard this voice calling my name and left the next day for the Himalayas.") to the sordid ("After six months of drugs and sex, I borrowed money from a friend and came home."). Intrigued by this process, some part of me scanned the horizon for a teacher. I waited in hope and confusion about the whole process.

JULIA HENGST, 23, IS A STAFF MEMBER OF *MANDALA* MAGAZINE.

Will I know him or her right away? Am I fooling myself and abandoning being responsible for my own life? It's a complex and challenging search, not at all common in the West.

What starts the earnest search for a spiritual teacher? Sometimes it is disillusionment. In Santa Cruz, California, a hotbed of liberal arts majors, many of the young people I know believe in the trust-the-universe-and-things-will-work-out philosophy, which encourages a lot of passivity and escapism. I tried that for a long time but nothing discernible happened. Sometimes it's the pain of having had nice clothes, nice cars, boyfriends, money, drugs, and a college education, but still no lasting happiness. I did set the intention at one point that I'd like to find a teacher if there was one, but mainly this "search" has unfolded in front of my eyes like a movie.

How do I recognize the person who will help me rid my mind of delusions and open my heart fully?

My first experience with a spiritual teacher was in junior year of high school in Santa Cruz. I had grown up in Houston, Texas, but when my brothers left for college and my dad moved to Hong Kong for his job, my mom blazed her own trail and moved the two of us to California. There she started walking her own spiritual path in Land of Medicine Buddha, a Tibetan Buddhist center.

I tried the local public high school for two weeks, but it didn't click. My mom and I researched other options, and I ended up at Mount Madonna School, an alternative education school that had only forty-seven kids in the high school the year I was there. On my first visit to check out the scene, two girls came up to my car as I was leaving and said, "Hi there. We heard you're joining the school, and we just wanted to say hi and introduce ourselves." This made such a warm impression on me that it didn't matter if everyone up there had strange Indian names like Suchitra, Sadanand, Badri Das, and Prakash. The academic program was impressive. Five kids the year before had gone on to Ivy Leagues. I think I got the "alternative school" part when, on the first day, they grouped us by our astrological signs and told us we'd have to stand up the next week and sing a song in front of the entire school.

The school was part of a community founded around an extraordinary Indian yogi named Baba Hari Dass (one of Ram Dass's teachers), a man who took a vow of silence over forty-five years ago and who teaches by writing on a small chalkboard. He was highly regarded as "the teacher" by students and their parents alike. This community was my first exposure to the teacher-disciple relationship in a spiritual sense. Up until then, the teacher belonged in the classroom and my role was as the class-clown. Respect for my teachers wasn't a priority.

I found the whole Hindu-yoga thing bizarre.

The new system came as a shock. I'd left Episcopal High School in Houston, where our parking area looked like a deluxe foreign car lot, and I was now in California, surrounded by a bunch of guru-groupies. Besides, I found the whole Hindu-yoga thing bizarre. For instance, one of the honored guests at the new school was an Indian yogi who wrapped an iron rebar around his wrists and had someone run him over with a tractor to show us the power of breath-control exercises.

I was sure Baba Hari Dass, the chief "guru," was a power-tripper. His students followed him everywhere like a herd. They used all their money to build his center. They asked him about decisions concerning their own lives as if they couldn't decide whether to wear red socks or blue ones— and it made me feel left out because I wasn't one of them. Couldn't they think for themselves? In my confusion and loneliness, I tried to find a solution in cigarettes, pot, and anything external that could distract me from my misery. My mom was trying her best to deal with me. With her background as a psychotherapist and her new tools from Buddhism, she had keen insight into what I was going through, but I couldn't hear any of it at the time.

Over the one year I was at the school, I started to listen to more of what Baba Hari Dass was talking about at his teachings on the *Bhagavad Gita*. He discussed karma, ego and egolessness, liberation and meditation.

I couldn't see any mistreatment or dishonesty in him. He was kind, patient, and certainly no slacker. To this day he pitches in and works on every project, from digging trenches to building walls—and he's in his late seventies!

I asked for an appointment with him, an option available to everyone for free. After meeting with him, I could clearly see that he knew things about me I'd never expressed to anyone. He asked me questions that catalyzed my own emotional and spiritual process, made me see my own self-destructiveness, and eventually led to greater clarity and understanding. It seemed like he could read my mind, and his mind-reading was more effective than any psychotherapy I'd tried in the past. Over time, I came to understand that I'd been projecting what I would have been doing if I were Babaji—I would have been power-tripping. After getting to know his students better and having more meetings with him in which he firmly, but with great kindness, confronted me about my habits of lying, smoking, doing drugs, I began to delve into spiritual and philosophical matters quite seriously. I felt especially interested in other Hindu-based teachers and in goddess worship. I also started to study yoga and Ayurveda, the Indian tradition of holistic healing. In time, it seemed that I needed something completely new, so I headed off for a year in India.

The longer I searched for my spiritual answers, the more my philosophical views fell apart.

While I was in India it seemed like the longer I searched for my spiritual answers, the more my philosophical views fell apart. I went to find God, but the whole concept of God dissolved the more I looked for it. I talked with anyone I could find: beggars by the roadside, Hindus, members of various other religious sects, zealous Palestinians, Zionists, displaced Africans. Everyone had ideas, everyone had questions, but no answers felt complete and trustworthy. Still without answers, I turned to familiar sources for my comfort: casual drugs, sex, and material pleasures.

At the end of a year, my mother invited me to meet her in Australia for a teaching by His Holiness the Dalai Lama. Aware that my life in India had become unproductive, and curious about the Dalai Lama, I agreed to meet her there. When I finally got to Australia and listened to the Dalai Lama, his answers were so down-to-earth, so practical and simple, that I couldn't get enough. I felt satisfied at last with some of the explanations I was hearing about why we're here, how we deal with suffering, what's the point of life. When I listened to him, I was "in the zone." It just hit home. Everything he said went to my heart. I was so impressed and deeply moved that I took refuge: I formally became a Buddhist.

Half of the healing was uncovering years of fear, anger, frustration, and depression.

During that same trip in Australia I met the man who would later become my main teacher, Lama Zopa Rinpoche. Recently, I asked a highly respected lama named Song Rinpoche, the reincarnation of my own teacher's teacher, how to recognize an authentic teacher. His reply: "If it's a real teacher, a qualified master, don't worry. They'll let you know." The classical teaching on this question is to observe a teacher for years, checking for certain things such as their concern for their student's welfare, their extensive range of knowledge, their unquestionable personal integrity and superior ethics. When these qualities meet in one person, and combine with their ability to open your heart and help you see things clearly, a faith is born that sustains a remarkable relationship marked by trust, courage, patience, and perseverance.

My relationship with my root guru, Lama Zopa Rinpoche, developed about six or eight months after I got back to the States, in mid-1997. This catalyzed a healing process for me. Half of the healing was uncovering years of fear, anger, frustration, and depression, and it often overwhelmed me to the point of tears. Lama Zopa came to a nearby Buddhist center and started giving a series of evening teachings. Even though I felt no strong enthusiasm, I decided to join my mom for a couple of evenings. Within a couple of days I couldn't stay away from his teachings. I don't even remember what he was teaching, but something kept pulling me back to him.

One morning I awoke and sat straight up in bed because of a pain in the center of my chest. I'd never felt anything like it before. I realized later that this was my heart, and I knew it had something to do with this teacher. This connection with him was opening it, stretching my heart in new directions, expanding my awareness of myself and others around me. I began to feel my heart on a regular basis, to see what opened and closed it. This lama was inside my heart and outside at the same time. He appeared in dreams. Sometimes I'd read a book and see a quote from Rinpoche that directly fit whatever experience I was having. I didn't consider any of this important until I mentioned it to other practitioners, who told me, "You have a strong connection with him. He must be your guru. Go talk to him."

I started asking his other students about him. I heard some far-out stories that captured my imagination. For instance, one student of his of twenty years told me she had been at one of his first courses in Nepal, and as her mind wandered away from what he was saying, she had the passing thought, "He kind of looks like a fish." A couple of minutes later, right in the middle of his teachings, he said, "For example, some people may think their teacher looks like a fish," and carried on without batting an eye. She looked around in surprise, but no one else noticed. He seemed to hear her thought like we hear music from the radio. Another student wanted to test the mind-reading abilities of another Tibetan, Lama Yeshe, so while he was teaching, he visualized offering a tall glass of orange juice to Lama Yeshe. As soon as the visualization appeared to the student's mind, Lama Yeshe stopped what he was saying, looked at the student and said, "Thank you dear, very nice," and continued his teaching.

I began to feel my heart on a regular basis, to see what opened and closed it.

I've since learned that the mind-reading tricks aren't important in Buddhism. Spiritual fireworks got my attention initially, opening the way for the real work of sloshing through my delusions. I went through a honeymoon period with Buddhism and the lamas, and decided I wanted to be a nun. Fortunately, Lama Zopa has more foresight than I do. When I told him about my idea, he said, "It is beneficial for you, but if you don't feel strong enough now, maybe you can wait three years and then decide." It's been just over three years now and I'm still not a nun, so I feel grateful for how skillfully he put it.

I've found it's important to be practical with my teacher, too. I need to think about what he teaches, and what he suggests I do. It's common in Tibetan Buddhism for teachers to give practices like one hundred-thousand prostrations, or one hundred-thousand mantras, and these practices take a lot of time. I've had to question why he would give me these practices, why I should do them, and analyze if there's been any change in my mind. I've come to respect a balance between reasoning and faith.

Sometimes, though, I feel like I don't need a teacher. I get frustrated that I can't just be a "normal" person who can live as I please without all my choices involving my teacher. But my teacher's guidance and care has helped me to become unstuck where I was completely stuck, and I feel closer to my natural creativity than ever before. My teacher didn't make this happen, but he's given me clear methods and an extraordinary example. He walks his own talk. I have to do the same thing.

I've come to respect a balance between reasoning and faith.

I've met teachers with totally different and unique styles. Some people have teachers who dance or paint, and others who are scholars and lecturers. The teachings say that if we really want to learn the Buddhist teachings, then a teacher will manifest according to our needs.

The Dalai Lama has said to check out a teacher for up to ten years to see if they're bona fide. If we can't check them for ten, then at least for two or three years. The more I learn about Buddhism and guru devotion, the more I respect the practicality of that advice. With Lama Zopa Rinpoche it happened organically. He would be in dreams, he would answer questions I'd been thinking about, and he would appear in visualizations where the Dalai Lama had been before. It was so strong sometimes that it increased my faith in reincarnation.

Sometimes it's been hard to maintain a commitment to any teacher. I've agonized about whether to go to teachings or to a rave with my boyfriend, and have drudged through guilt trips after taking drugs because I was sure I'd screwed up my spiritual life and my teacher would disapprove. There's no real black or white with this. Sometimes up, sometimes down. My teacher, at least, seems to remain stable no matter what I'm doing!

I've agonized about whether to go to teachings or to a rave with my boyfriend.

Just as any relationship unfolds, the journey one takes with a spiritual teacher is filled with unexpected adventures, delights, hardships, and turns in the road. It's life as usual on one level, but with my teacher I can measure my progress toward a more complete happiness and integrated personality. Am I doing better overall in my relationships? Am I acting according to the ethical behavior my teacher talks about and exemplifies? Can I handle turbulent emotions better than before?

The more I understand my own mind, the closer I feel to my teachers, not only Lama Zopa Rinpoche, but my teachers everywhere. Buddhism teaches that the outer guru is a reflection of the inner guru. This means that if I do my best to be a good person and work through my delusions day by day, and if I have faith that I have the same potential as my teacher, I will find the amazing qualities—love, compassion, humor, ethics, and wisdom—inside myself that I admire so much in Lama Zopa Rinpoche and the Dalai Lama. If I had never had them as examples, I probably never would have thought I had a chance to be like them.

part two

LIFE STORIES

INTRODUCTION

The small buddhist community where I lived put Zen and basketball together thirty years before Michael Jordan and Phil Jackson made it cool. As a kid, I sat on the hood of our blue VW Bug watching my parents and their friends take practice from the *zendo* to the parking lot that was their court: being totally spontaneous, staying in the moment, connecting nonverbally with the other four teammates, striving energetically and still letting go into the flow. In three decades, Zen basketball has gone from homegrown experiments to a widely understood integration of sports and the spiritual.

As the dharma has blossomed and matured in America, so too has a generation of born-and-raised Buddhists. What is it like to grow up in dharma communities or have Buddhist parents? Are there advantages to learning Buddhism from childhood? How does a teenager bring that learning into adult life? What are these kids doing today? What challenges have young Buddhists of convert parents faced in being part of a minority religion—sometimes viewed with suspicion—and how have they addressed those challenges? Are the experiences and issues of kids of convert Buddhists similar to those who come from Asian Buddhist cultures? Being conversant with two generations, in what ways can this small group be helpful to bridging older Buddhists to younger Buddhists? As both insiders and outsiders of mainstream American culture, what sorts of refreshing critiques of society can be offered? What perspectives would these Buddhists have about where Buddhism in America is heading and where it should head? This section touches on all these questions in the life stories of some children of Buddhism.

GROWING UP WITH THE DHARMA BUMS

Joshua M. Schrei

I GREW UP in a strict Zen Buddhist family in the '70s, a time when vegetarianism and Eastern spirituality were not nearly as commonplace as they are today. I was raised on brown rice and tofu and the sound of strange chants echoing through wooden monastery halls. My childhood was a blend of traditional Buddhist tales and ceremonies set against the bleak industrial skyline of Rochester, New York. It was a childhood of meditation and devotion, of serenity and compassion, but most of all, it was a childhood of great incongruities and cultural clashes, summed up perfectly by the two posters that occupied the walls of my bedroom, one boasting the serene visage of the Kamakura Buddha, the other the smiling face of Terry Bradshaw, quarterback for the Pittsburgh Steelers.

> ı was raised on brown rice and tofu and the sound of strange chants echoing through wooden monastery halls.

The Rochester Zen Center was on a tidy, tree-lined street in a quiet neighborhood. It had a backyard that had been converted into a Japanese garden, complete with a covered walkway and a magnolia tree that bloomed in the springtime.

My friend Jake and I were the heart of the small clique of Rochester dharma brats. The Zen Center was our stamping grounds. Many days

JOSHUA M. SCHREI, 30, IS A WRITER AND A POLITICAL ACTIVIST LIVING IN BROOKLYN.

There were spirits and ghosts in the unlikeliest of places.

we'd tear around the Japanese garden together, or save our pennies to buy Nectar Pies at the Community Co-op or carob shakes at the Lotus Café.

One Halloween, the Zen Center had a party. Jake and I and the rest of the dharma brat crew were gathered at the bottom of a stairwell, eating whole-grain cookies and sipping Japanese tea. Suddenly, without warning, several adults came running down the stairs. They were participants in the Zen Center Halloween play and were dressed in terrifying costumes—Japanese demons and hungry ghosts with snarling faces; the tormented spirits of the Buddhist world.

We screamed and ran helter-skelter, seeking refuge in the only safe haven we knew, under the golden Buddha statue in the *zendo*. Later, when the coast was clear, we emerged, slightly shaken.

It was like that, my childhood world. There were spirits and ghosts in the unlikeliest of places.

––––––––––

I was a vegetarian from day one, as were most of my Buddhist friends. Sugar and all forms of junk food were banned; totally off-limits. My parents and I did our shopping at the Zen Center community co-op, stocking up on soy sauce and bulk grains. When we occasionally ventured to more mainstream establishments like Star Market, I walked, wide-eyed, down aisles of colorful candies and syrupy sodas that I knew were forbidden fruit.

In conservative Rochester in the '70s, being vegetarian was unheard of, and so it was nearly impossible for us dharma brats to hide. We were doomed to be the subject of teasing and ridicule from the very first day of school. As soon as anyone caught a glimpse of our bag lunches—which were inevitably full of organic apples, dry and crumbly home-baked bread, and tahini sandwiches—it was over. Many times I tried to hide the contents of my lunch from other kids, not because I was embarrassed to be vegetarian, exactly, but more because I didn't want to have to explain myself.

I had to explain myself constantly. Every meal with out-of-town relatives, every restaurant that didn't have a vegetarian option, every school picnic or camping trip, I had to justify my vegetarianism and await the inevitable rebuttals and questions. Even if people approved, which they usually didn't, I was still "weird" or "unusual" or "different." The worst times were when I slept over at a friend's house and had to tell their parents that I was vegetarian. I knew that they wouldn't simply shrug it off, and I really didn't want to have to explain myself. In fact, I would do anything to avoid explaining myself, short of actually eating meat. So I dreaded dinnertime. As the hours ticked closer, I'd feel a knot growing in my stomach. I'd stall as long as possible. I'd hope that maybe, by some miracle, the meal would be meat-free and I'd be able to just eat it with no explanation. But that never happened, not in those days.

"Josh, we're having sloppy joes tonight, is that okay with you?" came Richard Bolt's mother's voice from the kitchen—the perfect, suburban, orange-and-brown kitchen, immaculate and spacious, with matching dishes and glasses with little yellow flowers on them.

I felt my heart sink.

"Uh, sorry Mrs. Bolt, I don't eat meat."

There was a long pause. Then came the inevitable question.

"You don't eat meat? Well, why don't you eat meat?"

It required a thorough explanation. I couldn't bullshit my way out of it. Sometimes I'd try to lie by saying I was allergic to meat, but that never worked. And I couldn't give the "health reasons" excuse back then. In fact, at that time most people thought vegetarianism was entirely unhealthy. They thought I'd grow up sickly and anemic, like some hollow-eyed veal calf. A few parents went as far as to accuse my mom of abusing me by not feeding me meat. Others said that it was the reason that I was so short. So more often than not, I had to give the full-on discourse.

"Well, Mrs. Bolt, my parents are Buddhist and they believe that killing animals is wrong."

There was another pause from the kitchen. I can only imagine Mrs. Bolt trying to process both the "Buddhist" part of my statement and the "killing animals is wrong" part.

"Well, honey, I've already made sloppy joes; is there anything else you can eat?"

"Oh, its okay, Mrs. Bolt, I'll just eat the bun."

Our vegetarianism was part of a larger worldview that taught us to be kind and compassionate toward all living creatures. As a child, I would be mortified if I saw a dead bird on the street. Jake and his mother went out in the streets after rainstorms to save earthworms from being stepped on. At school, when other kids were squishing spiders or lighting ants on fire with a magnifying glass, we would tell them to stop. When kids were fighting, we would try to break it up. And later, as we grew more comfortable with our Buddhist identities, in fifth or sixth grade, we'd give the kids who were engaged in bug-squishing or ant-frying moral reprimands and explain to them, very seriously, why it is wrong to kill, even little bugs.

———————

On lazy afternoons, I would sit up in the Zen Center library, lying on the carpet and inspecting the various books. Old hardcover editions of the Lotus Sutra, the sayings of Huang Po, or *Moon in a Dewdrop* by Eihei Dogen. And, tucked away in a corner, a small red paperback entitled *Zen Comics*.

I opened the book at random, thumbing through the simple, inkbrush cartoons, taking in the stories.

An old bearded master approaches his disciple, who is rapt in meditation.

"O Disciple," says the master, "Why are you sitting in meditation?"

"Because I want to become a buddha," replies the disciple, earnestly.

The master shrugs and says nothing. Instead, he picks up a floor tile from beneath his feet and begins polishing it furiously.

"Master, what are you doing?" exclaims the disciple, distracted.

"I am polishing this floor tile to make a mirror," says the master.

"How can polishing a floor tile make a mirror?" the disciple asks, confused.

"How can sitting in meditation make one a buddha?" replies the master.

———————

The particular style of Zen that the Rochester Zen Center taught, that of Harada Roshi and Yasutani Roshi, emphasized the attainment of enlightenment through hardcore practice. The young Zen students at Rochester meditated diligently, seeking *kensho*, the enlightenment experience.

For my parents, kensho was the great prize, the pie-in-the-sky, the Buddhist equivalent of winning the sweepstakes. It was a moment of perfect realization, when all would be laid bare and the true nature of mind suddenly revealed.

Zen stories are filled with vivid and enticing descriptions of kensho experiences. "I came to realize clearly that Mind is no other than mountains and rivers and the great wide earth, the sun, the moon, and the stars," says one man. Another wakes up in the middle of the night, laughing hysterically and proclaiming: "There's no reasoning here, no reasoning at all!" Yet another says: "I have it! I have it! There is nothing! I am everything and everything is nothing!" The experiences are dramatic. After years of hard work and several times

"when i grow up, i want to be a buddha."

almost abandoning hope, people wake up in the middle of the night, sweating. They are spurred on with the *keisaku*, the so-called "awakening stick." They seek, they seek…and at last! Kensho hits them. The way is clear.

I was curious about enlightenment, about kensho. The adults spoke of it so much I figured it must be very important. After meditation retreats,

I'd hear them talking to one another in whispered tones. "Did you hear? So and so had a kensho experience!"

It was so abstract, so hard for me to fathom. I wondered what enlightenment looked like, what it tasted like, how one could tell when it had happened to them.

Sometimes, I'd go to my little meditation cushion and sit for five minutes, following my breath the way my parents had taught me. When I was done, I'd wonder: "Am I enlightened now?"

Once, after listening to one of Kapleau Roshi's *teishos*, I asked my mother: "Mom, is Roshi enlightened?"

"Its not that simple," she replied.

Kensho was not only hard to reach, but impossible to describe once you got there. It wasn't easy, this enlightenment business.

As I grew older, I began to think about what to do with my life. At first I entertained all the usual childish notions of being a fireman, or an astronaut, or a football player. But somehow, even then, I knew that these were secondary. My real role in life was to be a spiritual seeker. All worldly options paled in comparison to the larger goal—enlightenment. I never even considered a normal life for a second; a blue-collar job as a clerk or a salesman, a career as a doctor or professor or stockbroker— how could this possibly suffice when the liberation of all sentient beings was at stake? Transcendence was imminent, delusions were ready to be rent asunder—there was no time to think of career or goals!

So when the question was popped by parents or friends or unsuspecting relatives, the all-pervasive, "What do you want to be when you grow up?" my answer was always the same:

"When I grow up, I want to be a buddha."

Not merely a monk or a meditation instructor or a Buddhist scholar, mind you, but the whole enchilada—a fully enlightened one, a never-returner, adorned in robes and emanating golden beams of light. Yes, I wanted to attain nirvana. What else would possibly do?

One day when I was ten, my friend Jed, a young Jewish kid with freckles and crazy red hair, came over to our apartment. After we'd exhausted ourselves playing tackle football and shooting off a water rocket in the backyard, I asked Jed if he wanted to play "Rebirth: the Buddhist Game of Liberation." Probably not having the slightest idea what I was talking about, Jed agreed. We went into my room, and I spread out the board on the floor.

The Rebirth board is a rather standard-looking gameboard divided into about two hundred bright, colorful squares. Each square has a symbol—usually a colored circle or a lotus—or sometimes even a little drawing of a landscape, or a palace, or the face of a Buddhist deity. Basically, each square represents a different realm of existence in Buddhist cosmology. There are several gruesome hell realms, which were endlessly intriguing for us kids, human realms, animal kingdoms, god realms, and buddha worlds; treacherous worlds populated by barbarian hordes; and battlefields of jealous gods. Each of these realms is a distinct and separate universe, with its own beings and its own set of experiences. What we do with our lives determines which of these realms we are reborn into. If we generate good karma, then we're reborn in the higher realms; if we generate bad karma, we are reborn in the lower realms.

"I was trying to give her enlightenment."

Jed and I played a lengthy game of Rebirth that day. I dutifully paused to read him the descriptions of the realms as we went and backtracked at a certain point to explain the whole concept of reincarnation. Then I extrapolated further about the principles of Buddhism. How Buddhism involves meditation and self-introspection. How Buddhism is nontheistic. In Buddhism, God isn't something that is outside oneself. It is attainable, reachable; one doesn't need a priest or a rabbi to act as intermediary. All it takes is a lifetime of dedicated practice and meditation.

At the time, I didn't consider how utterly bizarre it must have seemed to Jed to have a fellow ten-year-old spouting off to him about the complexities of Buddhism. Jed had probably never really thought about his Judaism or considered the intricacies of his own religion. But I had. And even more bizarre is the fact that I came to those conclusions myself. My parents had certainly never told me that Buddhism was better than Judaism. But somehow I'd just decided it was.

I can't remember if Jed went home and told his mom, but I didn't see Jed too much after that.

Years later, what struck me most about this botched conversion attempt was the degree of moral certainty I had, even at such a young age. I was completely convinced that Buddhism was the way—the only way—to salvation and was willing to go out of my way to prove it. And it wasn't just me—this type of righteousness was rampant at the Zen Center.

One day in elementary school, Jake pushed a little girl off a railing. Sobbing, the girl picked herself up and ran to get the teacher, who admonished Jake and asked him why he'd done it. The teacher probably expected Jake to confess or to lower his eyes or to give the standard "because I felt like it" excuse.

But Jake had loftier aims in mind. He looked up at the teacher and confidently replied: "I was trying to give her enlightenment."

There seemed to be a common belief floating around the Zen Center that we were superior to everybody else. The rest of the world was trapped in an endless cycle of ignorance, while the people at the Center were the privileged few who knew the way out of this cycle. The everyday world, in my memory, was a place that needed to be transcended. Day-to-day life was simply not enough. There was always a feeling of something else, just out of reach, that when attained would make everything all right.

This search for enlightenment was constant. A constant sense that "our lives will be better someday"—but not today. And our lives will be made better, not through the attainment of something tangible like "a good job" or "a house in the suburbs," but by the most abstract of abstracts: the attainment of enlightenment. We will be a better family through kensho. Not by missing one evening sitting and going to the movies for a change, but by going to the sitting and leaving me with the baby-sitter, again.

Even as a kid, I remember being a little confused and occasionally wondering where all this searching was going to get us; while other kids were being told by their parents: "Someday you'll grow up and have a family and a house and a two-car garage," I was learning about nirvana and goallessness. While other families had priorities like making money, advancing their careers, or getting their kids to go to the right school, my family dwelled in a world of intangibles, of abstractions, of philosophical concepts that do not translate easily into day-to-day life in the twentieth century.

> we will be a better family through kensho.

The Zen Center was so many things for me: A beautiful community, an environment devoted to love and compassion. A monastery with a rigorous practice schedule and an emphasis on enlightenment. A sense of tradition, and yet a sense of breaking with tradition as well. A place of fun and festivity, ritual and meaning, of moral tales complete with talking animals, flying *devas*, and good virtuous kings. Daily meals of whole grains and soy sauce. Occasionally, bagels, or a tub of strawberry ice cream, or the magical release of two hundred bright balloons. An elephant with six tusks. A gravel rock garden. A polished wood floor. The sharp knocking of a wooden mallet against the *han*; the indentation that the mallet left after years of daily use; the words inscribed on the wooden surface: "Life is passing quickly by. Wake up! Wake up! Don't waste a moment!"

Doubtless our tainted lens of hindsight will not see much difference between the practice centers of the late '60s and '70s and the later influx of pop-spirituality into America. But these were hardcore practice centers, traditional monasteries and ashrams that paved the way for future

American spiritual practitioners. To be sure, they had their faults, but to their credit the spirituality they taught was no fad. For me, in my memory, the Zen Center will always remain a chunk of the East suspended in time, a flowering Japanese garden inside a glass paperweight of the past, in which brown-robed students rushed to and fro, seeking the way.

Bridging East and West

Elijah Ary

AT FIRST GLANCE, I may seem like your typical Western guy: stressed-out over final exams, playing ice hockey in between papers, living in a normal apartment with my wife. But to my close friends, I am also known as a *tulku*, a reincarnation of a Tibetan Buddhist monk. Ever since I was "discovered" at age four by a Tibetan monk and then confirmed at age eight by His Holiness the Dalai Lama, I have tried to bridge these two parts of my life, Western and Eastern, Canadian and Tibetan, normal guy and honored person, ice hockey player and scholar of the dharma. It hasn't always been easy.

I was born in Canada in 1972 to a Jewish father and Protestant mother, who became Buddhist in their early twenties. I was conceived shortly following an initiation ceremony to Avalokiteshvara, the bodhisattva of compassion. A few years later, my parents opened a small dharma center in our home in Montreal, where many wonderful Tibetan monks came to teach the dharma. It was clear to them from the start that I was not your average kid.

to my close friends, i am also known as a tulku, a reincarnation of a Tibetan Buddhist monk.

Once, when I was about five, my father was playing with me and swinging me by the arm. I giggled and said, "I used to do that to you when I was your father!" A few years later, my father decided to teach me how to

ELIJAH ARY, 28, IS STUDYING TIBETAN LANGUAGE AND RELIGION AS A PH.D. CANDIDATE.

properly set up an altar. After bringing me in to the shrine room and explaining everything to me in detail, I asked him, "Why don't you move this bowl over here, and that statue over there?" Thinking I had misunderstood his first explanation, he repeated himself. When he had finished, I said "Yup...that's right," and walked out of the room.

my mom attributed these stories to the creative imagination of her sleepy son.

One day our family went to visit a local temple in Montreal to see a prominent Tibetan scholar visiting from India named Khensur Pema Gyaltsen. I remember looking up at this large man who emanated an austere yet warm presence. He had a beautiful smile that came from the deepest part of his being. I liked him immediately. When we got home, I began telling my mom that I had once had a teacher like Geshe Gyaltsen who was named Geshe Khunawa, and that he lived in a far-off place that only I knew how to get to. I told her of specific friends and of a protector deity in the form of a horse with wings. My mom attributed these stories to the creative imagination of her sleepy son. She nevertheless decided to tell my dad about my musings, and my dad mentioned it to Geshe Gyaltsen later that evening when he visited the temple again. To my dad's surprise, Geshe didn't think these were fantasies at all. On the contrary, he said he knew the people that I was talking about, but that they had passed away some time ago...in Tibet!

Khensur excitedly returned to India to research what I had said. Meanwhile, I continued to weird out my family by telling them stories of my regular interactions with Geshe Khunawa and other friends, whom I saw in dreams. But aside from this, I was a typical schoolboy. Four years later, in 1980, we received two letters from India. One was from Khensur Pema Gyaltsen, explaining that his research confirmed his suspicions: I was the reincarnation of Geshe Jatse, a Tibetan geshe from an important monastery in Tibet, who had died in the mid-1950s. The second letter, from His Holiness the Dalai Lama, explained that he had given my case personal attention because it was the first time that someone from the

Geluk School of Tibetan Buddhism, of which he is the head, had rein-carnated in the West and was of Western parents.

My parents were shocked, even though they believed in Buddhist tenets of karma and rebirth. Suddenly these theories took on very real meanings, and although they felt honored to have been blessed with such an unusual child, they also felt bewildered by the implications of the news. How should they treat me? What did it mean to parent a tulku? My sisters also didn't know what to make of it. To my older sister, I was more of a pest than anything else, and my younger sister just didn't understand.

Throughout my childhood I continued to show that I was unusual. On one occasion, I was brought before a renowned Tibetan Buddhist scholar, Zong Rinpoche, who had allegedly been a cousin of my prede-cessor, Geshe Jatse. He spoke no English. I sat down in front of this impressive, stern elderly figure, not saying a word for almost half an hour. I then got up, prostrated

The last time he had seen me, I was Geshe Jatse in my previous life.

myself three times, and left the room. My father was embarrassed, but then the teacher burst into laughter. Zong Rinpoche, translating through an attendant, said I hadn't changed a bit. The last time he had seen me, when I was Geshe Jatse in my previous life, I had come in, sat without saying one word for half an hour, got up, prostrated three times, and left. For this teacher, there was absolutely no doubt as to who I was, and he gave me a small statue of Tsongkhapa, the founder of the Geluk School, as a symbol of recognition. I have carried it with me ever since.

A third letter arrived not long after the first two from some exiled Tibetan monks living in a monastery in India. They were friends of the late Geshe Jatse and said that I belonged in the monastery with them in order to pursue my spiritual education. My parents were confused, because it suddenly seemed like it was a bad thing for me to be raised by them. We consulted many teachers, some of whom said that as a tulku I belonged in a monastery and others who said they didn't want to cause tension by giving any advice. One day my mom came to ask me what I thought. I told her that I wasn't ready to go yet, but since I couldn't resist my karma, I would have to leave one day for the monastery. Finally, my parents consulted the Dalai Lama himself. He said that I should go eventually, but I should focus on getting a Western education in the meantime.

My parents felt torn between being "good buddhists" and being "good parents."

School was the last place I wanted to be. I was clearly different from the other kids. Sometimes I talked about "my geshe" or the Potala Palace in Tibet, saying that it was my favorite place in the world. At recess, I wasn't interested in playing "war" or in fighting as the others were—though I did love playing hockey. I was constantly teased and sometimes even beaten up just for being different. In the classroom, I couldn't see how math and geography had relevance to my goal of attaining enlightenment, so I didn't put much effort into studying. The low grades on my report cards were often accompanied by comments like, "A good student, but we know he can do better," and, "He doesn't really try his best; he should work harder."

All this time, the monks in India continued to pressure my parents to send me to their monastery. They just assumed that Western parents would be as elated as Tibetan parents about their tulku son, and they were frustrated that my parents weren't complying with the standard way of raising a tulku son. My parents tried to negotiate by finding a place close to home where I could study Tibetan language and Buddhism, but that seemed to displease the monks even more. Under pressure, my parents sent me to places further away, like Vancouver, California, and even France. This didn't work either, because the resident teachers were often from other Tibetan Buddhist traditions and the monks in India objected.

Between all this moving around and missing my friends, family, and school, I got worn out and developed asthma. My parents had run out of solutions and felt torn between being "good Buddhists" and being "good parents." The stress began to tear wider the small rips from other marital differences, and they eventually divorced. By 1986, things had come to a head: I was no longer in school, my parents were living in different places, and everyone felt that I should either go to India and get the education I "needed," or else waste my life watching TV and waiting for my friends to come home from school so I could play with them. So in late October, I said good-bye to my dad and two sisters—one of the most painful experiences of my life—and set out for India with my mother, who stayed there with me for two months to help me settle in. It was there that I spent the next six years doing what I hated the most: studying.

Though I was sad to be leaving my home in Canada, entering the monastery in India felt like coming back to another home, a home I hadn't been to in a long time and had dearly missed. I formed immediate friendships with the monks, some of whom were Westerners who had been living there for many years. No one was teasing or beating me up now for being different; in fact, I was given special honors. Most importantly, I found myself completely absorbed by my studies. Learning about how the mind works, philosophy, meditation, debate, the Tibetan language, and memorizing texts and rituals often added up to fourteen hours of intense studying a day—and I loved it because this stuff seemed relevant, important, and worth learning!

Though I was sad to be leaving my home in Canada, entering the monastery in India felt like coming back to another home.

One aspect of my monastic training that mesmerized me was debate. A key component of the Geluk curriculum, debate hones logic and comprehension skills while deepening one's understanding of Buddhist thought. It is very physical too, and often looks like the participants are fighting when actually they are discussing the fine points of Buddhist doctrine. During a debate, one person is sitting and answering philosophical questions thrown at him at high speed by a standing participant while the rest of the classmates watch and listen. The examiner claps his hands together at the end of each question, soliciting an immediate response from his opponent. The examiner's right and left hands are said to symbolize wisdom and logic, and the joining of the two implies that the respondent must use both wisdom and logic to formulate a valid answer. When the debate gets interesting enough, other people try to participate, and the result is usually something that looks like a professional wrestling match. But there is no animosity between the participants, and the pushing and shoving often ends in laughter. From the moment I saw my first debate, I was hooked. I wanted to jump in, but I had a small problem: I barely knew Tibetan!

I grappled with the meaning of impermanence when my dearest teacher became very sick.

Underneath all the academic rigor was another addictive practice that I hadn't been taught in public school: meditation. Through calming and focusing my mind I was able to truly understand the most important lessons from Buddhism: lessons about impermanence, the nature of the self, and suffering. Meditation also made all the theory I studied for hours on end immediately relevant to real life. Especially, I grappled with the meaning of impermanence when my dearest teacher became very sick. When he died, I felt as though I had lost a part of myself and had a hard time believing he was really gone. On the suggestions of another teacher, who kindly showed me how to meditate more seriously, I began reflecting more on impermanence. Through the experience of my teacher's death, combined with meditation practice, I was able to understand better the transience of our fragile and precious existence. I realized that no matter what we do to avoid it, impermanence is omnipresent. But in contrast to this initially despairing thought I came to see that impermanence is what allows the world to be so beautiful. If things were everlasting, I would not take the time to notice the blossoming of a flower, the growth and unfolding of my friends and loved ones. We would not know the difference between suffering and pleasure, for either state would be perpetual. We would be incapable of change and thus of self-improvement. So I began to see that impermanence lay beneath all the different appearances in the world, and with this vision came a certain degree of acceptance of and nonattachment to life's evanescence.

After six years at the monastery, I found that I had become completely absorbed into another culture. Speaking fluent Tibetan, my English now sounded like my second language. The Tibetans didn't seem to notice my pale skin and nonflat nose and insisted I couldn't possibly be a Westerner. Being so accepted, I was allowed to penetrate deeper into the Tibetan culture than most people, and my whole world was their world.

But somewhere deep inside of me there was a Westerner who was beginning to stir. My life didn't seem as fulfilling as it should be, and at nineteen I began to contemplate my purpose in this world both as a Westerner and as a Tibetan. I was born in the West for a reason, I reflected, and that reason is to be a bridge between the Eastern and Western cultures. I felt an earnest wish arising within me to help people be free from suffering by showing the transience of this existence and the way to grapple with that by teaching about Buddhism and the Tibetan culture. Although my training told me that being a monk in a monastery brings much good to sentient beings, the Western side of me wasn't completely convinced. After consulting with the Dalai Lama, I decided it was time to leave the cloistered home of the monastery and return to the West.

My new life in Montreal put me in some culture shock. Living at home with my dad, I took up a job at a convenience store, worked at a skating rink, and started taking college courses for a degree in Religious Studies. I wasn't sure how or whether to explain to my friends why I'd been a monk in India. I cautiously revealed my identity to a few people. Some friends accepted it and thought it was cool, but some people seemed just as freaked out by it as when I was a schoolboy—only they no longer tried to beat me up. Integrating my two worlds was awkward and

> Deep inside of me there was a Westerner who was beginning to stir.

challenging. I often felt like I was acting my way through the "normal guy" routine, not being true to myself or to others.

It was in college that I began to feel like my bridge from East to West was beginning to take shape. I decided the best way to teach Buddhism was not in a dharma center where disciples would cling to my every word. I didn't want to be revered in that way. Rather, in the university I could more easily marry the valuable Western perspective on Buddhist Studies with the vastness of the Tibetan Buddhist tradition in the classroom. It allowed me to gain the outsider's perspective I couldn't get studying in the monastery and add that to my insider's knowledge, giving me a more complete understanding of Buddhism in the process. I also began making Western friends who were studying Buddhism too. In this setting, my dual identity has finally come into some kind of harmony. In the mornings, I still try to keep up a regimen of prayers and meditation like I did in the monastery, but my days are filled with classes in Tibetan texts, Sanskrit, Buddhist history and philosophy. And in my spare time, I still like to shoot a hockey puck around with friends.

Occasionally I will guest-speak in courses on Buddhism about my unusual childhood. The fact that I'm a Westerner seems to make my story more accessible to Westerners. I show that the dharma can happen anywhere, even in the West—it's not some strange, inaccessible thing only Asians can understand. That I play hockey and like Hollywood movies but also explore the depths of dharma gives people the possibility that they wouldn't have to give up their Western identity in order to practice Buddhism. The curious students pour out tons of questions at the end of my lectures. "Who are you?" "What is it like?" "Do you really believe you're a tulku?" In my answers I find myself bridging the foreign and the familiar through the dharma, as I had aspired to do eight years ago when I left India to return to the West.

EXTREME CARE

Jae-ho Lee

I REMEMBER AS A YOUNG BOY going to the monastery for the annual celebration of the Buddha's birthday. At six in the morning, I sat nodding away sleepily in front of the shrine, totally bored. For the many years that my family went to the temple, I couldn't understand why we were praying to a couple of statues with such devotion. Not only was the whole thing meaningless to me, but it was also tedious to sit there for hours, following the monks' chanting and dharma talk.

My parents were devout Korean Buddhists. My father's side of the family had been Buddhist for generations. My grandmother had built a temple in the Korean suburbs for public use in that neighborhood; it had been a family dream to build a temple. My mother was brought up as a Catholic, but she converted to Buddhism when she married my dad. She would go to the temple every week, while my dad, a successful businessman, supported the temple financially. Being brought up in a Buddhist family, I took for granted the temples, Buddha statues, monks, and prayers, not really thinking about why they were important or relevant to me.

> Not only was the whole thing meaningless to me, but it was also tedious to sit there.

My indifference to Buddhism changed when my father died in an airplane bombing in 1988. I was thirteen, and my father had been my whole

JAE-HO LEE, 26, RAISED IN HONG KONG, IS FOUNDER AND PRESIDENT OF X-TREME CARE, A HOME HEALTH CARE AGENCY IN NEW YORK CITY.

> The doctor recommended that I take prozac, but I decided to try meditating and praying.

world. I was in deep shock at his sudden death. I desperately wanted to know why he had to die and what happened to him afterward. Because I was so young, though, it was hard to make sense of it. I remembered that according to Buddhism everyone gets reborn. I prayed for him to be reborn into a better life, either on this earth or in the Pure Land with Amitabha Buddha. For the first time, something in Buddhism seemed to make sense and help me.

My father's death was also devastating for my mom, who had known life only as a wife and homemaker for so many years. She suddenly had to take care of two sons by herself, and she knew nothing about making money. Somehow she had the strength to take over my dad's company, quickly absorbing business skills, and making it a very successful business that supported all three of us.

Around that time, when I was depressed from losing my father, my mother introduced me to a monk with whom I soon developed a very close relationship. Reverend Hae Jong helped me understand, over time, why people need religion to live in such a fast-paced, hectic, and tragic world. He told me that good and bad things can happen at any moment in one's life. My emotions, he said, should not be extreme in either direction: don't be too excited by good news, nor too disappointed by the bad. I don't think I really understood what he was saying, but it was important to me that I could be close to this kind monk who cared about me.

It became clear a little later that I was having severe anxiety attacks and psychological problems due to the trauma of suddenly losing my father. The doctor recommended that I take some anti-anxiety medication, like Prozac or Ativan, but I decided to try meditating and praying instead, as Reverend Hae Jong suggested. The meditation did relieve the butterflies of anxiety in my stomach to some extent. Still, my mom and the reverend could see that I was really struggling.

Several years later, Reverend Hae Jong started to teach me about chanting, which I had considered the most boring aspect of the temple. He had me write the chants over and over again until I had them memorized, which was even more tedious than singing them. I did it more to please him than because of the chants themselves. I was surprised to find, though, that after some time what had seemed so boring began to free me from anxiety and calm my mind. I began to pray by chanting earnestly and more intensely as a way to move on from my father's death. And then, just at the end of each session, I chanted to my dad to watch over my mom while she went through this difficult time. I began to understand better why the monks spent so many hours a day chanting.

When I was eighteen, my mother planned a big pilgrimage with Reverend Hae Jong to Southeast Asia, where Theravada Buddhism thrives, and to where the Buddha lived in India. She wanted me to witness Buddhist practice in those countries so that I could understand Buddhism better. We first went to Chiang Mai in Thailand to the spot where my father's plan had crashed. We prayed there for a day. It was overwhelming to be in that spot, and all my pain seemed to rush back into my heart. I felt crushed and thought I couldn't finish the trip. We went on to India, where my mom and the reverend wanted to show me the suffering of others. I was shocked by the extreme suffering from poverty in Old Delhi. I had never seen such terrible things: some beggars didn't have hands or legs! It was said that some of them chopped off their legs or hands just to lure more money from travelers. Seeing so much misery made me realize how luxurious my own dilemma and suffering were. In the filthy streets, with so little to eat, somehow people continued with their daily lives. Children would even smile up at me. I began to see how fortunate I was, even though my dad had

I was surprised to find that after some time what had seemed so boring began to free me from anxiety and calm my mind.

died, and that I was being self-centered to continue mourning for so many years. I realized that my suffering wasn't unique, that all beings suffer. That, I remembered, is what the Buddha taught, the first Noble Truth: the truth of suffering.

However, just as I seemed to be getting a grasp of Buddhism in my life, another tragedy struck my family. A few years after that trip, I came to the States on a rugby scholarship to study at Boston University. My older brother Joung-ho also came to play rugby and study at a university in Pennsylvania. Everything seemed to be going well, until the morning of October 1, 1994, when I got a call from a hospital. The nurse told me that my brother had broken his neck in a minor rugby collision. He was paralyzed from the neck down.

I was absolutely devastated. I could not understand why another traumatic event had to happen to our family. All I could ask was *why*. Why should this happen just when we were all moving on from the pain of my father's death? More bad news came: the doctor said that recovery wasn't possible; all we could do was wait until medical science improved, or for a miracle. It took me two days after my brother's injury to get up the courage to break this news to my mother. I was afraid she would not be able to stand her own son's deep suffering. She arrived from Hong Kong two days later with Reverend Hae Jong. I almost couldn't bring myself to look at her face, but when I did, I was surprised to see her calm and collected.

This tragedy challenged me as a Buddhist. I frantically looked for an answer about why this had to happen to my brother. I thought about what Buddhism says about karma. But it didn't seem fair to say that my brother had gotten paralyzed because of bad karma from a past life. For several days and nights, I watched Reverend Hae Jong praying by my brother's bedside without talking to anybody. I urgently wanted an answer from him, but even he couldn't give me answers. I think he was in such a deep shock himself that chanting was the only way to survive looking at my brother's limp body. Without answers, I took a firm resolve to take care of my brother for the rest of my life. My mother had to return to Hong Kong to keep the company running so that we would have enough money to pay for the staggering medical bills.

After my brother had been at Penn State Hospital for a month, we moved him to Mount Sinai Hospital in New York City. I dropped out of college and began a daily life centered on my brother's care, day and night. I was the only one he could depend on. My personal life was set aside completely, and I spent most of my days alone by his bedside. I used to be the baby of the family, not having to worry about a thing. Now I was expected to be the pillar of strength.

After two years of dedicating every moment to caring for my brother, I began to wonder if I would ever have a life of my own. My mom wanted me to keep taking care of him, but I wanted to go back to school. I didn't know what was the right thing to do. I began to feel depressed and worried that my life would end like this. And things weren't so great between my brother and

This tragedy challenged me as a Buddhist.

me: because we never had time to ourselves, we got on each other's nerves. He kept second-guessing all my behaviors and would get angry with me when I didn't do things the way he wanted. I began to resent him. He was frustrated that, once an independent and healthy young man, he was now completely incapacitated and totally dependent on his little brother. I just wanted to get away, even for a moment.

Every day our relationship seemed to get worse. My anger toward my brother and mother intensified. What about *my* life? Do they ever think about *my* welfare? Then I would get angry with myself. *I am so selfish!* It is my duty to devote myself to my brother. I felt overwhelmed and burdened by the whole situation, by the whole world it seemed. I felt like I was going crazy.

Around that time, I met a monk who was just a few years older, Reverend Il-mee. He lived at a temple I visited outside New York. He must have picked up on my misery because he asked me if I'd like to travel with him. Such a departure seemed impossible to me, but Il-mee persuaded my brother to give me just one day off to go fishing. My brother reluctantly consented because he respected this monk.

We went to the seashore off Long Island. We spent the whole day and well into the night fishing. I finally had the chance to talk to someone about my dilemma of needing a life of my own but feeling bound to care for my brother through my mother's wishes. Il-mee advised me to find a life of my own. He said, "Don't sacrifice your life that way! If you really want to help your brother, you have to find a way other than being the puppet for your brother's hands and legs. Without finding your own path and happiness, you won't realistically be able to carry your brother's burden. Otherwise, your unhappiness will just be another tragedy in your family." I asked him about how a bodhisattva is supposed to do what I've been doing out of compassion. How can I have my own life without that being selfish? He continued, "The bodhisattva tries to make circumstances better at every moment through compassion. But if you make yourself miserable, then you aren't being compassionate to yourself. And your misery will affect your brother, and that is also not compassionate. It's not that you should abandon your brother to pursue your own happiness, but you need to find some other solutions that will make you both fulfilled. Don't get stuck in passive karma." We did not catch any fish, but I had caught some very valuable wisdom.

Encouraged by his advice, I hired more nurses to take care of my brother while I returned to school at Hofstra University and excelled in my studies. With the instruction from Il-mee, I began meditating regularly. He told me, "Just keep your mind on the moment you are in, not in the past or the future. Sit back and reflect on yourself." In these quiet moments, I realized that I was clinging to the pain from the past and creating anxiety about future pain. Seldom was I in the present, and when I was, I was so locked up with fear of pain that I was immobilized. The meditation also cultivated in me a sense of interconnectedness. I began to realize that I wasn't the only person in this kind of situation, but that other families have to deal with the tragic injury of a loved one. They too have to deal with home care, finding good nurses, frustration with them-

> But if you make yourself miserable, then you aren't being compassionate to yourself.

selves, their loved one's own inner pain, and so on. Once I understood how I was stalemating myself and that my dilemma was not unique, what I should do with my life began to clarify. I discovered the project that would not only make me happy and use my education, but also take advantage of my experience in caring for my brother, provide him with care, and help other families.

The idea for X-Treme Care, a home health care agency, came out of my own experience. Very few other agencies had had the trained nurses to deal with my brother's severe disability. I realized that to improve the level of care I would have to do it myself. I decided to dedicate my life to setting new standards and procedures in the specialized area of spinal cord injuries.

X-Treme Care renders specialized home health aid services. On the surface, physical assistance such as turning the patient in the evening to prevent bed sores or moving limbs to prevent joint stiffness looks simple, but it's not. In addition to special training with excellent nurses on this level, the aides in my company are also given training in psychology. Psychological training is, in my mind, more important than the physical because of the anger and suffering the patients are enduring. Care at this level is the basis of religion: just learn to genuinely love the person and really care from the bottom of your heart. Believe it or not, a little bit of love will enable a patient to recover much faster. We are also imple-

In these quiet moments, I realized that I was clinging to the pain from the past and creating anxiety about future pain.

menting a new idea in which new patients can send in a videotape of their daily routine. We then show the videotape to the home health aide so that they can get custom training and become familiar with the patient even before they have entered their home.

Starting this company has brought everything together for me. I am doing something with my life that makes me happy. I am providing my brother with the kind of quality care that I feel good about. And I am helping relieve the burden for other families who are in similar situations, as well as helping give other spinal-cord injury patients a higher standard of care.

I am grateful to my brother because he has made me become a much stronger and better person. If it had not been for my brother's inspiration, I would not have even thought about starting this agency. In this sense, he is a bodhisattva who made my situation better at last. He played a big role in helping me start this agency by advising me on how to provide the best care for clients. I have learned from him that it only takes a little bit of affection and love for the patients to make them feel more comfortable and at ease. Having chosen this occupation has made me feel at ease with myself with the conviction that I can contribute to society, my family, and myself.

As a Buddhist, my father's death and my brother's injury made me become a person I never could have imagined. After a long time as a naïve Buddhist, these two tragedies made me question my faith and learn from it. I now feel like a baby bodhisattva, who's learned from other great bodhisattvas like Reverends Hae Jong and Il-mee, my mother, and brother, taking his first steps in a new world.

A Dharma Punx Path

Noah Levine

M<small>Y PARENTS WERE DEEPLY INVOLVED</small> in spiritual practice while I was growing up. They told me stories from the Hindu and Buddhist traditions instead of reading to me from Disney books. My heroes were Hanuman the monkey king and the Buddha, although I was also fond of Ravana, the demon king. Sometimes, I secretly cheered on the armies of Mara. I was aware that my parents were involved in some sort of practice where they would sit up straight for hours, in silence, with their eyes closed. My siblings and I would say, "They're sleeping sitting up again." We were never forced to join them or go to teachings or to the temples. Meditation was their thing, and although it certainly influenced their parenting, it was never a direct part of my upbringing. I do recall certain teachings about letting go of anger and softening to pain; when I look back, I see that these were subtle ways of sharing the dharma with us kids. But I didn't realize this at the time.

By junior high school I was getting loaded on an almost daily basis.

At a very early age I began experimenting with drugs. By junior high school I was getting loaded on an almost daily basis with speed, acid, and any other drug I could get. I smoked and drank heavily. I started listening to punk rock music and started to reject my parents' spiritual path. I

NOAH LEVINE, 29, LIVES IN SAN FRANCISCO, WHERE HE TEACHES MEDITATION BOTH IN THE COMMUNITY AND IN PRISONS, AND IS WORKING ON A BOOK CALLED *THE DHARMA PUNX.*

saw meditation and the lot as hippy garbage and for weak-minded followers of some Asian god. I resonated very deeply with the angst of punk and the political messages being delivered in the music and the scene. My involvement in the punk scene deepened the rift between my parents and me. My father later told me that he used to throw away my T-shirts that said "Fuck Authority" or had pictures of violence on them; I always just thought a friend had stolen them. My teen years were filled with sex, drugs, and vio-

on that retreat I realized that I had finally found what I was looking for in all those years of drugs and booze: moments of freedom from dissatisfaction and moments of peace.

lence. I was in and out of Juvenile Hall on a regular basis from age twelve until eighteen. The drug use got heavier and heavier, and by the time I was sixteen, I was completely strung out on crack and booze, stealing to support my habit, and fighting to maintain my image of being a hardcore punk. By the end of my drug use I had traded in my Mohawk and leather jacket for a crack pipe.

At seventeen, I was locked up in Juvenile Hall looking at another felony, possibly facing seven years in prison. Filled with fear and regret, two things happened that changed my life forever. Talking to my father on the phone, he suggested a simple mindfulness meditation practice of being with the breath. I was hesitant but willing, and in my cell I experienced, for what seemed like the first time ever, the miracle of mindfulness. Through watching the breath come and go I was able at moments to be present and let go of all the fear of what was going to happen at court next week and all of the regret and condemnation for my past actions. The other thing that happened that time in Juvie was that I began attending Twelve-Step meetings to address my addiction.

After about nine months in Juvenile Hall and a group home, I turned eighteen and was released, sober, in therapy, and trying to meditate once in a while. The first couple of years were pretty rough; I was still lying, stealing, and manipulating. Between scrawling graffiti and fighting, I would now and then come back to the breath and practice mindfulness. At two years sober I got in big trouble for graffiti and hit a spiritual bottom. Looking at going back to jail, I felt I had nowhere else to turn but to spiritual practice. It was the only thing that seemed to give me any relief from the constant feeling of dissatisfaction.

I began working the Twelve Steps and instantly found some freedom in prayer and meditation. It was at that time that I also began sitting more regularly and attended my first residential retreat, a weekend with Jack Kornfield and Mary Orr. On that retreat I realized that I had finally found what I was looking for in all those years of drugs and booze: moments of freedom from dissatisfaction and moments of peace.

Being an addictive type, I quickly became a die-hard spiritual practitioner; when I find something that feels good, I want more of it. Of course meditation practice doesn't always feel good, but I knew that it was the only thing that would take me to the place that I wanted to go in the long run. I had seen it work for my parents and many people around me in the Twelve Step programs. Early on in my practice I began contemplating monasticism, wanting the highest realization possible. With the willingness and youthful enthusiasm to set my sights on enlightenment, the robes seemed like a viable option. This was also influenced by my second retreat that was led by the English Theravadan monk Ajahn Amaro. Although a bit intimidated by the austerities and renunciation of the Theravadan tradition, I was deeply inspired by his presence.

I ended up taking a personal vow of celibacy while continuing to live the life of an American punk-rocker.

Around that time I connected with a non-Buddhist teacher and ended up taking a personal vow of celibacy while continuing to live the life of an American punk-rocker, while hoping to eventually go to Asia for ordination. Practicing mindfulness on the cushion, at work and in the slam-dance pit, I began to incorporate my practice with my lifestyle. After a couple of years I fell in love, broke my celibacy, and ended up leaving my teacher, who was no longer practicing what he preached. That relationship was quite challenging, and we were off and on for a couple of years.

During one of our breakups, I packed a bag and headed for Asia with my two closest friends. Before I left, I found out from Jack Kornfield where I could ordain and which centers to visit. That pilgrimage was not one that ended in robes, as I had expected. Instead, it ended with my ex-girlfriend joining me in Nepal and us returning to the States together. I began to let go of my intention to ordain and started to see my path as being in the world and of being of service to my fellows and my generation.

All of my actions have always been aimed at finding happiness.

A couple years later, while doing the "Year to Live" practice, I hit the road again doing retreats and visiting sacred places. I returned to Asia and went to Mexico and Central America. Practicing as though I had only months to live, I completed all unfinished forgiveness and made sure that everyone in my life knew how much I loved and appreciated them. Preparing for "death," I attempted to let go of ever having a family, of ever getting enlightened, and of ever teaching.

At the end of that "Year to Live" practice, I began teaching meditation with my friend Soren Gordhamer in the same Juvenile Hall facility where I had begun practicing ten years earlier. As I let go of everything, it all began to fall into place. I returned to school, completed my undergraduate degree, and began a graduate program in Counseling Psychology. I was offered a job teaching meditation and dharma to teens and families at Spirit Rock Meditation Center, and I helped get a Rites of Passage program started at the San Francisco Zen Center. I began working on my book, *The Dharma Punx*, which tells my story and looks at how I and others have transformed the punk rock ethic into deep spiritual exploration.

Reflecting on my life's journey thus far, it is clear to me that all of my actions have always been aimed at finding happiness; whether it took the form of addiction and rebellion or dharma practice and service, my intention has always been to find freedom.

In My Father's Footsteps

Hojo Tone

I WAS BORN AND RAISED in one of the Shin Buddhist temples of Waka-yama, Japan. Although my older brother has inherited responsibility for the leadership of the Tone clan as a Shin Buddhist minister, I also decided to become a Shin Buddhist minister.

I was born and raised a minister's child. From the day I could talk, I learned to follow Shin Buddhist practice, reciting the *Nembutsu*—*"Namu Amida Butsu"*—and studying, learning, following, and practicing the Buddhist way of life, without having any doubts or questions about it. As a child, I merely recited the Nembutsu without any depth of under-standing. In chanting, I always asked for something, such as, "May I pass the test!" "May I receive a nice birthday present!" "May I have good luck!" I thought that Amida Buddha, Buddha of Immeasurable Light and Life, would grant my wish. The Nembutsu was always emphasized throughout my

> I had regarded Amida Buddha as a superman, and at that time my thought was only to rely on Amida Buddha as the ultimate power.

upbringing, but with the passing of years, many questions arose within me. Why do I recite the Nembutsu? Is it just because that's what I've been taught? Do I really recite the Nembutsu sincerely and whole-heartedly? I discovered I needed to answer these questions for myself.

HOJO TONE, 31, IS A GRADUATE STUDENT IN THEOLOGY AND AN ORDAINED JODO SHIN-SHU MINISTER OF THE HONPA HONGANJI MISSION OF HAWAII.

Then, in high school, something happened that changed my life and began the journey to answer these questions. My father suddenly had a heart attack. He was forty-nine years old. As soon as I heard the news, I hurried to the hospital. The doctor told me that it was doubtful that my father's life could be saved. Shocked by what I had heard, I went home to my temple, not knowing what to do. So, I put my hands together and bowed. I said, "Please help my father," and recited, with all my heart, "Namu Amida Butsu, Namu Amida Butsu, Namu Amida Butsu…." I had regarded Amida Buddha as a superman, and at that time my thought was only to rely on Amida Buddha as the ultimate power. Several days after the heart attack, somehow my father regained his health.

Around that time, I was fortunate to be selected as a member of the YBICSE (Young Buddhist International Cultural Study Exchange) delegation from Japan. That was the last time I saw my father. My father died on the day that I left for the United States, but I didn't know that then. When I came back to my family temple in Japan about three weeks later, I was informed of his death for the first time. Suffering and in pain, my heart was heavy with grief. For me that experience truly seemed like Hell.

For some time I found it difficult to get over the loss of my father. For the first time I began to consider seriously the question of what it means to be a human being. I also began to think deeply about the meaning of Amida Buddha and the Nembutsu in my life. Half a year after my father died, my mother showed me my father's last words written moments before he died. I carefully read them page by page. On the last page my father had written, "Namu Amida Butsu." And in his last breath he had said to my mother, "Amida Buddha came for me; I will go back to the Pure Land of Amida Buddha. See you again." Regarding me, away in the U.S. as an exchange student, my father had instructed my mother, "Do not call him back, because he has his own future." Hearing these words, his deep faith, I was inspired to become a minister.

So although I was born and raised a minister's child, and had "practiced" the Nembutsu from my earliest childhood, I began actually *living* the life of Nembutsu only thirteen years ago. I learned from Shinran Shonin, the founder of Jodo Shinshu Buddhism, what the Nembutsu truly is, and I became determined to become a minister. While I was a student at Ryukoku Daigaku, the Shin Buddhist University, I received a scholarship for two months of overseas research on temple activities on the U.S. mainland and Hawaii. During my visit, I spent about two weeks at Honolulu Honganji under the guidance of the head minister, Rinban Reverend Hoashi. At that time, I met a woman, a member of the Women's Organization of Honolulu Honganji, who kindly encouraged me to return to Hawaii when I became a minister. As strange as it may seem in retrospect, it was the conversation I had with her that made me decide to do just that.

A true encounter with the Buddha's teaching means we are growing up.

On February 20, 1996, I arrived in Honolulu to become a Honganji Buddhist minister, and I came to Hilo Honganji on May 21, 1996 upon receiving my assignment from Bishop Chikai Yosemori. When I came to Hilo Honganji, I had an interview with Dharma School children. They asked me why I became a minister.

I told them that I think that the Buddha's teaching is crucial to developing and forming our character and our way of living. A true encounter with the Buddha's teaching means we are growing up and living in the path of Nembutsu, Namu Amida Butsu. *Namu* is my isolated, solitary self, and *Amida Butsu* means I am embraced by boundless compassion. My life, thus, is a gift that is granted me, and I want to share the gift of well-being for all people through ministry.

Ever since I lost my father I have been seeking the deep meaning of the Buddha's teaching. But for many years my studying to seek spiritual knowledge was only at my desk, through my intellect. It was only through meeting my teachers and through the influence of many others like my father that I could realize my inner truth. As a minister, I want to embody the Buddha's teachings and affect the lives of others as I have been affected by such dear friends. Ever since I received Namu Amida Butsu from my father, I have found my true self, or awakened to myself, through that teaching. Namu Amida Butsu is my life.

My Mom's a Buddha

V. Sharif Fennell

To me, she is the personification of what it means to be a buddha in daily life. Her name is Marionette, and she is my mother, teacher, mentor, and friend. In October of 1974, when I was barely two years old, my mother took refuge in Nichiren Daishonin's Buddhism. In those years, my family was struggling just to get food on the table. My mom was the single parent of two very young and energetic boys, my brother and me. We lived in Roxbury, a borough of Boston that was a very rough place to grow up in the '70s. She had just decided to come off drugs and shape up her life. But things were still desperate for our family, and in those early years sometimes all she had was the support of her Soka Gakkai family and her faith in Buddhism.

she inspired me to hold onto this chant as the pillar supporting everything i did.

I don't remember how old I was the first time I chanted *Nam-myoho-renge-kyo*. I remember not quite understanding it but knowing that my mother had a deep passion for this chanting. She inspired me to hold onto this chant as the pillar supporting everything I did. Every morning and evening, without missing a day, the three of us chanted *Nam-myoho-renge-kyo*, which is the title of the Lotus Sutra, and then recited the second and sixteenth chapters (*gongyo*) in front of the *Gohonzon*, a scroll with

V. SHARIF FENNELL, 27, BORN AND RAISED IN THE INNER CITY OF BOSTON, IS CURRENTLY APPLYING FOR MEDICAL SCHOOL.

the Japanese calligraphy of the sutra. The dedication to practice showed in my mom's life. She began finishing her college education while often holding down two jobs. Not only did she work hard for our family, but she also pushed me to perform at my best at all levels, especially at school. I was often placed in accelerated programs, working with deaf students and learning sign language from watching the other children.

It was the chanting that pulled her out of the downward spiral that many of her friends did not survive.

As I got older, I gained more faith in this form of Buddhism. The event that really glued me to chanting happened when I was ten. I had been in a gym class that got the chance to go to the Junior Olympics in Indianapolis, Indiana. The long drive from Boston seemed unending, so I passed the hours by chanting the gongyo. I didn't know what my teammates would think of this, so I said it under my breath. I knew that my coach and teammates didn't really think I should have made the team, but to their amazement I was able to capture two gold medals in Tae Kwon Do. I don't think I could have done that without a deep trust in the chanting. This was my first real evidence of the power of gongyo.

My mom not only pushed me to be successful, but she also helped prevent me from getting sucked into the inner city's problems. In my neighborhood, between crime, drugs, and the foolishness and arrogance of youth, some of my friends didn't make it out alive. Being a victim of the '60s drug era, my mother knew firsthand the carnage drug abuse can leave in its wake. She had struggled for years to rid herself of drug addiction. But it was the chanting that pulled her out of the downward spiral that many of her friends did not survive. She would say to me, "People who take drugs are always trying to escape something." My mom had decided not to run away from her problems anymore but to honestly face them. It was through her faith in the Gohonzon and her assiduous practice that she surmounted her obstacles. Seeing her transform her life instilled in me a confidence that many of my Roxbury friends lacked.

I remember the first time I was offered alcohol. Because of the confidence my mom gave me, I was boldly able to say simply, "No." But the fact that some of my friends smoked pot and got hooked on alcohol didn't deter me from hanging out with them. After countless futile attempts to lure me into the same practice, they ceased their attempts. With my Buddhist practice, along with my mother's guidance, I was able to develop a solid sense of self that shielded me from these kinds of peer pressures.

It was also through her actions that I came to understand how to truly care for people. My mom's care of her friend Margaret was the best example for me of real love for those in need. Margaret, like my mom, was forced to raise two children on her own. She had little money and even less hope, which often left her grasping for answers. Marionette would gladly lend an ear and chant with Margaret as though the problems were her very own, in a genuine effort to find a viable solution. Margaret would come over to my mom's apartment just to chant, to study Buddhism, and to find solace in my mom's friendship and faith in her. But it wasn't just Margaret and me and my brother that my mom's heart encircled. There were countless others who flowed in and out of our home, which was like a haven for them. My mom often didn't always have answers to people's problems but would instead compassionately protect and support whoever needed it, using prayer and study to resolve whatever obstacle.

But she still had plenty of attention for me. Seeking a better education for my brother and me, my mother enrolled me in a bussing program that sent me to a suburban school so that I could get a better education. One of the major drawbacks was that this school was an hour away. I

> My mom often didn't have answers to people's problems but would compassionately support whoever needed it.

had to get up very early in the morning in order to chant *daimoku* (that is, *Nam-myoho-renge-kyo*) and do gongyo. Many times I did gongyo and chanted quietly in the back of the school bus. The school was in a nearly all-white town north of Boston. Being from the city and being black, it was hard to fit in at times. But I was taught through Buddhism that we all inherently possess a buddha nature, and thus we are all equal. Because of this I was more able, I think, to be myself and not force myself to fit in, and this attitude came naturally. I made several friends as early as first grade. I would often stay the night with friends from Melrose. From first grade right on through my senior year in high school, I was able to befriend people from very different backgrounds. Still, I never had to change who I was or sacrifice my beliefs to fit in.

My mom continually challenged me to challenge myself in school. Perhaps my biggest challenge was my love for football. I was not as advanced as the rest of the kids on the team by any stretch of the imagination. But through sincere prayer and tremendous effort, I was able to go from a freshman who didn't play a single game to a starting senior. Junior year my coach asked me about what I wanted to do for college. I let my heart pour out to him. I had fallen in love with the sport of football. I told him I wanted to play football in college. I thought maybe I could play at a Division I college, the most competitive. I also told him that I wanted to go to medical school. All this, after a junior year of record low grades and barely playing junior varsity, the coach, holding back a laugh, told me flatly, "You could not clean the showers at a Division I school."

Remembering my mother telling me there was nothing I could not accomplish with Buddhism, I began to chant even more vigorously than before. I threw myself further into Soka Gakkai activities. I also began to work extremely hard at football and my studies, missing very little practice or classes. The result was a drastic turnaround in my grades, from C's and D's to nearly all A's. I practiced all summer long to start on the varsity team. Much to my dismay, the first game of senior year was a day away, and I had prayed and practiced so hard seemingly with no results. I went to my mother feeling very discouraged. She told me to never give up and to have faith, and she reminded me that no prayer to the Gohonzon goes unanswered. She recounted a quote from Nichiren Daishonin's writings to one of his disciples, "The journey from

Kamakura to Kyoto takes twelve days. If you travel for eleven, but stop with only one day remaining, how can you admire the moon over the capital?" These words were to encourage a disciple of his to persevere until the end. Lo and behold, the first play of the first game of the year, the starter in front of me got hurt. In I went and I never came out, starting the remainder of the games for that year and playing much better than anyone ever expected, including me.

At the end of the season, my coach convinced me that if I really wanted to play college football, maybe I could play Division II or III but to get Division I out of my mind. He also felt I could use another year of prep school following gradua-tion. I then reiterated my original goal and held firm that I neither wanted to play for a small school nor wanted to go to a prep school. I ended up at UMass the following year, a Division I school. While I was there, I went from barely making the team as a freshman, not sure how to pay for school, to a senior co-captain, all-American, on a full athletic scholarship, and an honor roll student. Now I am preparing to take the MCAT, the admission test for medical school, this April and hopefully will go on to medical school.

> "The journey from Kamakura to Kyoto takes twelve days. If you travel for eleven, but stop with only one day remaining, how can you admire the moon over the capital?"

I have come a long way by watching and learning from my mother. Earnestly practicing Buddhism with her my whole life has allowed me to spread my wings and fly. Lucky for me, it has all just begun—I have my whole life ahead of me. Armed with a passion to make a difference in the lives of people everywhere, as I saw my mother do, I know I cannot fail.

LIVELIHOOD

INTRODUCTION

ONCE I WAS VISITING the office of a Buddhist publishing house. While making a cup of tea in the kitchen, I noticed a poster of the serenely meditating Buddha near the drying rack. Just below him were two large dispensing boxes: one with minipackets of Pepcid AC antacids and the other with Bayer aspirins. I laughed, reflecting on the challenges of bringing the ideals of Buddhism into the whirlwind that is our educational and professional lives.

Young Buddhists today also search for ways in which Buddhism provides a foundation in the work world. How is meditation useful for someone who programs computers for long hours? How does a young social worker use the bodhisattva path to understand the true meaning of helping another being? In what way is Zen foundational to working as a hospice staff member facing death day in and day out? This section looks at how young Buddhists integrate dharma with employment.

In a similar vein, many young people are deeply searching for ways to integrate the dharma with life beyond the usual job, beyond the temple, beyond the cushion. Some ask: What good is all this meditation, chanting, bowing, reading, and talk if it's only for myself? How does inner peace truly affect world peace? How can this seemingly self-centered spiritual journey speak to poverty, social injustice, crime, oppression, disease, war, the environment, extinction, the effects of natural disasters, globalization, the World Bank? This section also addresses, in part, the fledgling movement of socially engaged Buddhism as young Buddhists express it.

Still other young Buddhists see Buddhism itself as a way to address social and environmental problems. These people are discovering professions as meditation teachers, university professors, chaplains in hospices and hospitals, and temple and community administrators. How do they see teaching meditation to incarcerated teenagers as addressing problems in our nation's justice system? How does a temple monk handle a suicidal member through the dharma? Why do these young professionals see Buddhism as an efficacious remedy for contemporary ills? We turn to these narratives in Livelihood for some thought-provoking reflections.

If a Nice Jewish Boy Sits in a Cave, Does He Make a Difference?

Seth Castleman

WHEN I WAS SEVEN or eight years old, my father would take me around our neighborhood collecting signatures calling for a bilateral nuclear disarmament with the Soviet Union. Together we walked door to door on the wooded, suburban streets, my father making an impassioned speech and asking people to sign his petition. We were living in an age of potentially imminent doom and destruction; how, my father asked, could one sit by and not act?

Mostly I remember the fact of going more than the details of the experience, yet there is one house on Partridge Road, less than a mile from where I spent my childhood, that I still picture clearly to this day.

A small balding man about forty came out of a modest home. As he listened to my father's spiel, he nodded patiently, periodically smiling down at me. But when it came time for him to sign the petition, the man became noticeably uncomfortable, shifting his weight between his feet and tapping his hand on his thigh.

i wondered at the time what it was about helping that made people feel so human.

"I can't sign." There was a long pause. "I...I work at Lincoln Labs. We,

SETH CASTLEMAN, 27, IS A WRITER, STORYTELLER, AND TEACHER. A PRACTICING JEW AND A STUDENT OF THERAVADAN DHARMA, HE WRITES ABOUT THE PEOPLE, PRACTICES, AND MYTHS OF THE JEWISH AND BUDDHIST TRADITIONS.

um...do research and development. Government contracts." His voice dropped. "I'm sorry." My father looked at him a moment, then smiled and said all right, thanking him for his time. We turned to go. We were half way down the slate path to the gate when the man called out to us.

"You know..." We stopped and turned. I remember the man looked terribly sad.

"You see all those bird feeders?" he asked. He pointed to a number of simple wooden structures hanging from the maple and oak trees in his yard. "I built them myself. I feed all the birds; from all over they come to my yard. You know, there are some birds that come to Lexington now because of my feeders."

I looked at the wooden boxes. My father nodded.

"Please don't think badly of me. Really, I try to make a difference."

We walked through the gate back onto the road, heading toward the next house with our petition. I wondered at the time what it was about helping that made people feel so human.

While my father spent his energy trying to stop the Bomb, my mother raised money for health care and education in the Third World. Over the years, our family marched down Main Street, Pennsylvania Avenue, in front of the UN building in New York, and even through Red Square in the first peaceful political demonstration since before the Communist Revolution. My siblings and I were raised to believe this was not only a sociopolitical response to suffering but also a religious one. As American Jews, to heal the world was as much a religious priority as prayer. My own activism went in stages, from animal rights as a teenager to social work with disabled, disturbed, and abused children in my early twenties. Then I found the dharma.

what they needed at the most basic level
I struggled the most with giving.

With sitting practice, it became all too apparent the degree of inner conflict that was at play in my mind, and I saw healing and insight as prerequisites to helping anyone. The social work required patience and compassion, two things I often felt I had in very short supply. As my meditation practice developed, it was clear how my own unhappiness, and the dissatisfaction and wanting that grew from it, was the barrier of separation between me and the children. If I was angry, needy, filled with self-judgment, or otherwise dissatisfied and self-absorbed, I had little room for the people around me. In moments— or even hours or days—of anger my patience dropped, my voice gained an edge, my concern for their well-being was lost behind my own self-absorption. These shortcomings became a source of even more unhappiness when I realized how these children—many of them victims of sexual or physical abuse, others merely neglected and unwanted—simply longed for loving attention. What they needed at the most basic level, I struggled the most with giving.

I heard an old yiddish voice kvetching, "so this is going to help the world?"

In fact, I saw my own unhappiness not only as a barrier to being of service but also the very motivation for engaging in service to begin with. My efforts were driven on some core level by a need to be loved and approved of through identification with my role and accomplishment. Not unexpectedly, as such external acknowledgment came, my longing only grew stronger. My doubting mind questioned the validity of such conditional sentiments—appreciation and acceptance based on behavior seemed dubious. As well, my limitations became clear when I saw that the real motivation to being of benefit was self-justification, the salving of my eternal inner wound.

Dharma practice became increasingly central to my life, and social service less so, until eventually at twenty-five I left to travel and practice in Asia. At the time, I was unclear whether I was leaving to do nothing or to learn how to do something more effectively. All the same, Asia was where it happened; the freedom option, the homeless potential, where wisdom was gained along with giardia, malaria, and a disdain for American materialism. I heard the words of my teacher ringing in my ears, "Free the mind. You can do no better in this life than to free the mind." But I also heard an old Yiddish voice kvetching, "So this is going to help the world?" I told my mother I wasn't dropping out; I was taking an alternative Ph.D.

Soon after arriving in India, I went to hear the Dalai Lama teach on Shantideva's text, *A Guide to the Bodhisattva's Way of Life*, in Bodh Gaya. At the teachings I met a young American man who had recently begun his dharma practice with a well-known Tibetan teacher at a nearby monastery. After the morning session with His Holiness, we walked together to the Tibetan tent-city, which had sprung up around the village, in search of lunch.

"What's your practice?" the man asked me as we stepped into Mohammed's, reputed to be the best noodle joint this side of Lhasa.

"Theravada," I answered. "Vipassana meditation."

He stopped just inside the tent flap and looked at me in the dim smoky light. "Oh."

Considering his tone and expression, he might as well have said, "Oh. I am so sorry."

Over *thukpa* and yak butter tea, I asked what he had heard about the Theravada, and after some prodding, he reluctantly explained.

"Our teachers told us how the lesser path does not lead all the way. Hinayanists are only in it for themselves. They get enlightened but don't take the bodhisattva vow, so they then don't help anyone else. What's the point of practicing if you don't go on to help?"

Beneath my initial anger and resentment, I had to wonder if there was not some ground of truth to what he said. A stark image came to mind.

I could not help but realize that my defensiveness was in part due to my own doubts that my practice benefited anyone but myself.

It was as if this man and I, both parched and beleaguered, met on a road through a vast and arid desert on our way toward an oasis. I am carrying a flask tied to my belt so that I may draw water from the well and quench my thirst. He, however, is trudging through the desert balancing an enormous stone basin on his head. When we arrive at the pools, I dip my bottle and drink my fill, then lie down to rest under a great oasis palm, sleeping happily in the shade. He, meanwhile, fills his basin and then, without even a sip for himself, begins dragging it back across the desert to bring water to every sentient being he can find.

Sitting there at lunch, I covered my pangs of inadequacy with self-righteous indignation that he was being judgmental and sectarian. While I tried to explain the merits of vipassana and its practitioners—failing to maintain much equanimity in the process—I could not help but realize that my defensiveness was in part due to my own doubts, doubts in my motivation, doubts that my practice benefited anyone but myself.

facing his demons once again when the medication wore off, he jumped from a train in paranoia.

That night, sitting on my cushion at the Burmese monastery in Bodh Gaya, I recalled the title of a recent book written by a Zen student-turned-rabbi, *One God Clapping.* I arrived at my own Jewish *koan:* If a nice Jewish boy sits in cave, does he make a difference?

After a month of silent retreat in Bodh Gaya, where the Buddha attained awakening, I traveled on to Sarnath, where he went next to give the first teachings. He too had struggled with questions of engagement versus seclusion. Upon enlightenment, the Buddha retired to his metaphoric cave, as he saw no point in trying to make a difference in so broken and deluded a world. Only the pleadings of the Brahma king, Sahumpati ("O Lord…there are those with but a little dust in their eyes"[*Majjhima Nikaya*, 26.20]), drew him forth to Sarnath to set the wheel of dharma in motion.

While Buddha walked, I went by means of bicycle—an old iron contraption, weighing at least thirty-five pounds. I named her Samsara, as she went round and round and caused me a lot of suffering. She had a propensity for breaking down every three kilometers. But as this is the nature of the Indian cycle; there was a roadside shop every four kilometers or so, a man on a brick with a pile of greasy tools and a pump, leaving me not far to walk each time. Given the lack of gears and the weight of my pack, I did not travel much faster whether she worked or not anyway.

Halfway to Sarnath, I encountered Wils. A German man of thirty-five, Wils had a long history of psychosis. He had come to India to meditate and free himself of the anti-psychotic drugs that kept him stable but deeply numbed and confused. Facing his demons once again when the medication wore off, he jumped from a train in paranoia, leaving behind his pack and all his pills. I found him semi-conscious on a steel gurney in the barracks of a small town hospital.

Wils and I spent the next week together, as we made our way to Varanasi and then Delhi, toward medical care and sanity. "I just want to be happy," he told me in one of his more lucid moments. "But I think it is very clear: that is not an option." Over the days, I held his hand, washed his body, and listened to his tormented story. I came to see that our sufferings were not so different, as we both longed to free our minds of old habits. "Why," he asked me, after almost throwing us both out a third-story window, "Why should I want to live? Is there anything here but suffering?"

Through it all a sincere love developed between us. But slowly and insipidly my ego took over the patient care, gaining in size with every meritorious deed. We said good-bye on the runway of a tiny airstrip, where I tied him into a two-seater plane with torn strips of my Indian shawl, sending him off to a German hospital. "It has been quite a week, Wils. I feel blessed to have met you." My mission was now complete. He looked up at me, scared and alone. Then he spat in my face. Even if I was not ready to face my pride, Wils was happy to confront it for me.

From there a long and painful journey unfolded, through the subcontinent, through the Himalayas, the forests of Burma, and the mind. The seasons passed in cities and villages, in meditation centers and monasteries. I traveled slowly onward on Samsara, wandering, wondering, waiting for nothing to happen. I crossed borders and recrossed. I climbed mountains and swam in the holy Ganga. I kept 227 precepts and fasted for forty days. And through it all I seemed to only care about myself more than ever before. Again and again, as I delved deeper into practice, identity dwindled and the familiar shore would move out of sight. With a mix of fear and guilt I would careen my rickety boat back toward land, trying to accomplish something wherever I turned. Whether it was finding Wils or someone to love or attaining insight on the cushion, more and more I saw how my efforts were less motivated by love than by ego-wanting. "Everything rests on the tip of motivation," the Tibetans say. I was only too clear that my motivation for action was rank with defilement.

While living as a monk in Burma, I had thoughts of spending my life there, practicing in my hut in the bamboo forest, yet time and again my koan played in the back of my mind. I was caught in the middle, neither out of the world nor engaged in it. My practice went through a particularly difficult period, rife with doubt and aversion, physical and mental *dukkha*, and deep waves of despair. One of my teachers pointed up to the great mountains surrounding the monastery. "You see those mountains?" he asked. "There are countless caves up there where monks sit and practice. Whether day or night, every moment of every day, there are monks sitting and practicing *metta*. They are sending loving-kindness," he poked his finger at

There were little old ladies who fed me soup while giving unsolicited advice or knitting me socks. "Grandma," I wrote home, "the world is filled with Jewish mothers."

my chest. "To you. Remember, you are always loved. Metta is being sent to you, so much so that it is like you are being held in the arms of the Buddha. Do not forget it, I tell you, lest you squander this great gift."

Over the months, I met countless kind and generous people who took me into their homes and put rice in my bowl. There were little old ladies—Indian, Nepali, Burmese, Thamong, and Naga—who fed me soup while giving unsolicited advice or knitting me socks. "Grandma," I wrote home, "the world is filled with Jewish mothers." Yet it is the gift of those nameless, faceless yogis in their caves that has remained with me to this day.

Upon returning to the U.S., I moved to a dharma center in the woods of New England for a three-month retreat. The first weeks were agonizing, as I faced my sense of failure and unworthiness in every sitting. I was back in America not engaged in the world but as confused and self-absorbed as ever. I tried practicing metta, but in my suffering all I could wish for anyone was sympathetic misery. Standing in my own shadow, I longed for acknowledgement, or if nothing else, a judge and jury outside my own mind.

yet sitting there in her beam of metta, I was at loss for words.

I went for an interview with Sharon Salzberg, one of the center's guiding teachers. In the little room above the meditation hall she was waiting, resting easily in a chair with a cup of tea. As I sat down she smiled. It was not her lips, but her entire being that smiled, and the metta she exuded was palpable, as if the arms of the Buddha were reaching out to embrace me. "So how is it going?" she asked, her eyes twinkling with delight. I knew she had asked this question over ten thousand times, but clearly she meant it. A dozen times that day I had practiced my report in the silence so that it would sound impeccable, adding just the right amount of progress, humor, humility, and spontaneity. Yet sitting there in her beam of metta, I was at loss for words. I had come into the room just as I had entered every room in my life, looking for acceptance and acknowledgement—or if nothing else, affirmation of my worthlessness. Yet she was offering the love I sought, not because my practice was worthy or because I had been of service to anyone or because I was funny or sharp or good-looking or kind, or because I was mindfully slow when I sat down. In that moment of stillness, on the edge of a wooden chair, I was receiving love and acceptance merely because I was the human being sitting in front of her. Never had I felt so recognized.

Over the next months, something slowly began to shift. It was as if after a very long time in the darkness of a cave, I had emerged into a beautiful garden. Slowly my ego's grip began to loosen. The self slipped away, as did the experience of body and mind, leaving only awareness itself. "Who am I?" arose in the mind again and again. With every answer there was a clear knowing, "I am not that." I saw all my actions in the world, all the people I loved, my hopes and fears and emotions. I saw myself as a child and as an old man. I looked at the body, the mind, and then awareness itself. None of it, clearly, was me.

> I saw myself as a child and as an old man.

In the space of this stillness bubbled forth immense joy and love. I giggled out loud in the lunch line and fell over laughing in the woods. I looked at a hundred silent faces and fell in love again and again. Each time I sat down on the cushion, I took refuge in the Triple Gem, and there arose the dedication, "May my practice be to serve all beings." For the first time in my life, I was identified with nothing, and underneath it all I found love.

In this state, I felt little desire to move back out into the world. There was so much joy and generosity to be found in the stillness that I was reluctant to let it shatter. "Go out and do something for the world," Sharon urged me as my retreat ended. So after leaving the meditation center, I went to New York City to teach vipassana to incarcerated teenagers in prison. I could not help but notice that, with this new role, ego and identification returned once again.

For my first class I had a group of twenty young men aged sixteen to nineteen. The youth sauntered into the prison classroom warily, their beige jumpsuits rolled up to show bulging biceps sprinkled with gruesome homemade tattoos. They talked loudly and eyed me suspiciously.

The prison director had warned me that J-Block was a difficult and aggressive group, but I was less afraid of conflict than I was of failure. I realized my accomplishments in the world or on the cushion meant nothing to them, and looking around the room I had no idea what I would say.

Remembering Wils, I asked, "How many of us want to be happy?" A few guys chuckled and someone cracked a crude joke, but eventually everyone nodded or raised their hand. "Alright, and how many of us are happy? How many of us don't suffer?" No one moved. Each calm face belied the suffering in their lives. "So our work is to be able to sit with whatever is happening, whether it is happy or difficult." Together we took a vow not to move our hands until the bell rang, and for fifteen minutes these young men, normally raucous and edgy, sat silent and still with postures erect, facing their moment-to-moment experience.

As eyes slowly opened, the room full of tough guys was now suddenly filled with little boys, lost, scared, and alone. The biggest guy in the group, in for murder, had tears running down his cheek. "It's my momma," he said, looking around to make sure no one was laughing at him. He wiped his face. "I can't stand that I'm in here, leaving her alone. I should be caring for her. I want to tell her I am sorry I'm not there." Another boy spoke quietly of going to court again and again, but no one there cared that he was a kind and decent person. Tattooed on his arm in big letters was written, "With only God as my judge."

We sat for a while not saying much, respecting each other's pain. In the silence I now had the answer to my koan. The practice for J-Block at Bronx Juvenile Hall was my practice as well: just sit. They did not care whether I knew anything about meditation or even whether I wanted to help them, but simply: Was I sincere? Could I sit with their pain; could

I sit with my own? For most of my life, while practicing dharma, or trying to help others, or dealing with pain and loss, I had seen right action
as a movement forward, an effort to change what was not right. Yet perhaps, instead, making a dif-
ference is much simpler
than that. It is the courage   could I sit with their pain; could I sit
to stand still. In the face of   with my own?
suffering can we not turn
away, nor need it otherwise,
but remain steady in the face of whatever arises? Like the moon on open
fields, the heart holds this floating world. And the movement to serve
comes not from grand aspiration, but the still, quiet voice of acceptance.

CAUGHT IN INDRA'S NET

Hwansoo Kim

S HE IS WEEPING AND I am watching her. We are in a Starbucks coffee shop, but nobody notices her tears. She blurts out her many dilemmas between sobs and says she can't deal with them anymore. For three hours I sit, just listening to her, trying to comprehend the reasons for her dilemmas. I notice in my peripheral vision that the coffee shop has four tables, and there are just a few people enjoying their late-afternoon coffee. One girl, who seems to be a student, is so engrossed with studying, several thick books spread over the table, that she forgets her coffee. Two others sitting together at a table seem to be a couple. They are busy showing affection to each other, as if the man were leaving for a long journey abroad. And then there are the two of us, the monk and the crying Japanese woman. Outside, it seems to be getting colder, the day ending, people drawing their collars up against the wind and hastening home. I feel the warmth of the coffee radiating through the doubled cups into my hands as I listen to her and at the same time feel everything around me. Floating above her voice is a strange music I've never heard. It sounds like a blend of modern and traditional Asian music; the plaintive melody resonates and magnifies the depth of her sorrow.

She says that before she was married she had dreamed of coming to Boston, the city of her hopes. So for eight years she scraped together some earnings to come here and study English. But she sees now that the dream is different from the reality. She did not expect loneliness, a wors-

HWANSOO KIM, 29, HAS BEEN A MONK IN THE KOREAN TRADITION SINCE HE WAS SIX-TEEN AND IS A STUDENT IN DIVINITY SCHOOL.

ening relationship with her husband, and mistrust from even her most intimate friends. All this, she says, sabotaged her dream and knocked her down in one fell swoop. My mind chews on her words, wondering why she takes these things so seriously and lets herself get out of control. Her tears don't stop. She keeps the already soaked handkerchief to her eyes and nose and won't look at me.

My heart twinges a little at her pitifulness. But in my deep mind, I am not able to feel the pain she has at that moment. After a long explanation about her dilemmas, she pauses and looks at me and waits, waiting for my words, for which I am not prepared. I have to force myself to say something. I say, as empathetically as I can, that she should not take her dilemmas so seriously, that time will heal it, and that she should wait and see and just focus on her studies. In spite of her sorrowfulness, I feel calm and still and tranquil. It is like a meditation: she and I in a coffee shop with wonderful music; people studying and loving each other; the sky darkening this world that he may take a rest after his work. The whole is in my mind and my mind is in the whole. Her dilemma is netted to this whole, so this dilemma is not a dilemma anymore. The pain she is feeling is related to everything, and as a result it is not anymore a dilemma, but a part of the whole. I remember a line from one book I'm reading for a class in Buddhism, that the whole world is "built on the image of Indra's Net, in which each node of the net is a jewel which reflects every other jewel." The net results of all these thoughts, curling on themselves while she speaks, come to a terse reply to her teary and expectant eyes: "Don't attach yourself too much to your dilemma," I say.

My loose and ill-considered advice has an unanticipated effect on her.

My loose and ill-considered advice has an unanticipated effect on her. The next thing I know, she begins talking about a friend of hers who studied here several years ago. He loved to walk along the Charles River, but one day, without explanation, he killed himself by leaping off Memorial Bridge. I shift my legs and straighten my back, looking closely at her. She

says it happened around this time of year. Suddenly my fantasy of interconnectedness, the reverie I have been entertaining for the last hour, dis-
integrates. My heart begins pounding as I watch the net of Indra become cut into smaller and smaller pieces, until she becomes the smallest

мʏ heart is swept with pain—
hers and mine, for all we have suffered.

particle. I feel her pain in my deep mind, this tiny jewel in Indra's net. My
mind races: What should I do? How can I pull her out of this deadly way
of thinking?

All the spinning thoughts about Buddhism and enlightenment and
compassion lose their power in the face of her words. I am speechless to
say anything that will recover her self-confidence. I begin to slide into the
misery of my own childhood, the death of my sister and mother, the terrible loneliness, my father's alcoholism. I start to tell her these things, and
as I do, I begin to feel her sorrow. My heart is swept with pain—hers
and mine, for all we have suffered.

We just look at each other, feeling the depth of the grief. Nothing to
say. We throw away our cold cups, pull on our coats, and start out the
door into the lamplit night of the Cambridge streets. As she turns her
back to leave me, I suddenly stop her, turn her around, and grasp her two
hands. "You are not alone. We are all related. If you kill yourself, it means
you kill your friends and your parents and me too, because we are one
body." She just nods and turns away. That night, she called me and said
she had realized that I was right.

HALTED BREATH

Amy Darling

IN THE DEPTHS OF MID-WINTER MAINE, during my final year of college, a close friend of mine from high school drowned in a river in India. Clutched by an initial wave of shock and pain, I folded in on myself, on the floor of my apartment. Tears flowed. The breath entered and left my chest shallow and halting. When I surfaced and found my lungs again, I settled into a very deep quiet. In the days and weeks following, I found myself healing Tyler's death, weaving that loss back into my life, with a surprising degree of acceptance. The experience opened a window for me, a window through which I could see my own impermanence vividly, like blinding sunlight. Rather than his death initiating a flood of questions, fear, and uncertainty, I found quiet.

> I committed to trying it at least three times before making any decisions about this "zen Buddhist thing."

A month after Tyler's death, I learned that a Zen meditation group met in the basement of a home two blocks away from my apartment. I began sitting with the group once a week. I committed to trying it at least three times before making any decisions about this "Zen Buddhist thing." That was in February of 1996. I'm still sitting.

During the first year and a half I sat *zazen* (sitting meditation), I har-

AMY DARLING, 27, WORKS IN THE BEREAVEMENT PROGRAM AT PROVIDENCE HOSPICE OF SEATTLE AND PRACTICES WITH LOCAL SANGHAS IN THE RINZAI AND SOTO ZEN TRADITIONS.

bored many questions about whether or not I could really do it. Despite the witness born by so many dedicated American practitioners, I wondered if I had to be Japanese. I thought maybe there was something genetic, something about being a young white, American woman that would prohibit me from "getting it." During my first lengthy meditation retreat, through the teaching of Zoketsu Norman Fischer, through the earnest and dedicated practice of the others participating, and through hours of zazen, it became clear that I was the only thing separating me from this practice. I realized there was nothing else hindering me from making a commitment to this path; that it was all right there. I sat at that retreat three weeks before leaving on a one-way ticket to Nepal. Among the many things in my backpack and pockets, I tucked the intention to continue my daily meditation practice and to carry that practice off the cushion into my daily life.

Among the many things in my backpack and pockets, I tucked the intention to continue my daily meditation practice.

————

The first time I went to Nepal was during my third year of college. Having experienced the most tremendous happiness there, I was determined to return. I wanted to hold that joy again, puzzle out how much of it arose because of my surroundings, and how much of it I could find or cultivate in myself. Upon my return a year later, I found that joy, and found it inextricably interwoven with myriad other experiences.

Less than an hour outside of Kathmandu (twenty minutes by foot, another half hour by bus) a small, two-story mud-and-brick house stands nestled among other homes and sculpted terraces. Nepalis come from three remote districts to seek refuge in that house. They come walking, with complaints of dysentery and skin conditions. They come on the backs of others, their bodies wasted by tuberculosis and cancer. They come hoping to find a place to sleep, eat, and get help navigating the health care system in Kathmandu. I spent a year operating that house with one co-worker. Together, we learned to meet the varied and challenging needs of those who arrived on our doorstep.

Before leaving for Nepal, I considered seeking out a teacher or community in the Kathmandu Valley to support my meditation practice, yet I created mental obstacles between myself and the Buddhist traditions most prevalent in Nepal. I hungered for the sparse aesthetic of the Japanese-style meditation hall. Rather than reaching out to learn what I could by embracing the traditions of Buddhist practice in Nepal, I honored them from a distance. Each morning I sat zazen in my bedroom, located right above the outdoor tap stand where my landlord washed his face and cleared his sinuses loudly. I set aside that time to quiet and open myself to each day.

I carried a *mala*, used it to bring me back to my breath in moments of impatience and frustration at the hospital, on the buses, and striding through the old bazaar. I visited Bouddha, one of the major Buddhist *stupas* in the valley, each week. Elder Sherpas and Tibetans shuffled along the smoothed stone path and whispered mantras with malas in one hand, prayer wheels in the other. My heart swelled each time I joined the sea of people circumambulating. I took refuge in the writings of Dogen, Shunryu Suzuki Roshi, and Maura Soshin O'Halloran. I also began to see lessons all around me: my own impatience and inappropriateness; the humbling process of becoming more skilled in a foreign language; and my fluctuating ability to be present with the suffering of those entering our house. Each patient became my teacher.

A fistula had developed from her intestines out into several open wounds on her back, through which pus and feces were excreted.

During the spring, our patient load doubled. As soon as we sent two patients home, three more arrived. We didn't have enough plates. People slept beneath frayed mosquito nets on the covered porch. Bhuwan, my co-worker, and I were worn ragged.

Palgi Sherpa arrived at our house in late spring, her forty-year-old body emaciated and frail. A palpable mass, the size of a small child's fist, sat prominently several inches below her sternum. A fistula had developed from her intestines out into several open wounds on her back, through which puss and feces were excreted. The mass in Palgi's abdomen was malignant. There were no choices, no chemo, no operation. The doctors dismissed us, offering only aspirin for Palgi's physical pain. We, in turn, had to discharge Palgi from our patient house.

I sat with her loneliness.

Her family did not believe she would survive the journey back to her village. They reluctantly took her to a tiny, single-room apartment in the city where they left her frequently alone. They were afraid of this woman whose body had become so ill and "dirty." The morning she left, tears streamed down her sunken cheeks. A mass, as solid as that in her own abdomen, settled in my stomach and festered.

After her move, I visited Palgi every two to three days. I cleaned the sores on her back. I made us tea and bought her groceries. I believe the most important thing I did was simply sit with her as her body deteriorated. I sat with her loneliness, listened when she wanted to talk, sat in silence when she didn't. Early on, I visited to resolve my own guilt, that lump in my stomach that came from having to send her away. But the guilt waned. In its place a deep gratitude arose. I felt honored to sit with this woman as she prepared for death. For me, there was no catharsis. Each time I sat holding her hand simply reaffirmed that my own body was no different than Palgi's.

————————

One Friday evening, the heat of late May hanging languid in the air, Bhuwan and I were called down to our patient house. Limp from a grueling week, I rounded the corner of the house to see Bahadur, a patient with a drug-resistant strain of TB, writhing on his back, his arms flailing. He was hollering at people we could not see. Tension spread from the base of my spine throughout my entire body. I was afraid he would die there, at the door of our house, and inspire fear in our other patients. His nephew, Pravin, took him to the emergency room. I surrendered to the idea that Bahadur would not come back. He died of cardiac arrest and drug-induced hepatitis the following night.

I met Pravin at the hospital the morning after the death. Together, we went to collect Bahadur's body. Inside the morgue it was cool and smelled stagnant. We found Bahadur's body wrapped in white gauze. Pravin picked up his shoulders. I wrapped my fingers around his tiny ankles and we lifted his body. I thought it would sag in the middle; I expected his tiny body to be unwieldy. It was stiff, like a pine board, dead not even twelve hours. I gazed at his shape through the gauze, thinking about the words we had exchanged two days ago, thinking about the voice that had come from this body, now silenced. We moved him to a stretcher, into the back of a "dead ambulance," and headed for the pyres of Pashupati.

I stood and observed each detail, mildly numb, pensive, humbled by how our bodies burn as quickly as wood.

I remember the heat of that day, that time of year before the rains come to cool the earth and fill the terraces. I learned to walk slowly on such days. That morning moved slowly with me, giving me enough time to absorb every detail. I had walked by the pyres a dozen times, always covering my mouth, choking on the smell. However, I had not before witnessed the cremation of any of the patients who died during my work. I felt a need to lay Bahadur's body to rest, to see a body just like my own reduced to ash.

Fifty feet away another cremation was in process. One rigid leg stretched out of the flames, muscle and skin remaining from the knee socket down. I stared without shame. As the sons of the deceased attempted to push the leg back into the blaze, that corner of the pyre collapsed. The leg tumbled to the ground. With some difficulty, they pushed it back into the flames with a lengthy bamboo pole. I stood, dumbstruck, as this human leg was pushed around like another piece of bamboo.

Pravin lit a small piece of wood and circled the body three times. He pulled the gauze back from his uncle's face, set it on his lips, and recovered the face sending a ribbon of smoke into the air, like a visible, final breath. The fire was lit. Long wet grass was laid on top of the body. As the flames leapt upward they caught his hair first. It sizzled and coiled in on itself, blackened. I was overwhelmed by an almost childlike fascination with every detail. I did not cry, nor did I feel mournful. I saw this as Bahadur's healing.

The fire consumed the flesh on his legs first, and eventually the attendant used a long bamboo pole to bend the legs back onto the abdomen. Occasionally he would bring the pole down hard on the body, gaining a sense of what was left. When the legs were no longer bone and tissue but smoke and ash, the body was carefully rotated using the pole—no lurching, no falling limbs. Bahadur's skull and abdomen faced down into the earth, eating the fire.

I stood and observed each detail, mildly numb, pensive, humbled by how our bodies burn as quickly as wood. It took only three hours for his body to be reduced to ash and swept into the creeping Bagmati River. There was nothing left, not a bone, not a piece of hair, not a fingernail.

I witnessed palgi's fear in the face of her own death.

I walked away from Bahadur's cremation. I took a bus into the city to visit Palgi. Arriving at the bottom floor of her tiny apartment building, I paused and steadied myself, cheek and palm pressed against the cool cement wall. I shut my eyes for a moment and breathed more deeply than I had since the quiet of my morning zazen. I could smell the infection while walking up the stairwell toward Palgi's room. I had walked away from death and was walking again into death. We sat quietly after I explained where I had come from. That day, it was she who held my limp hand. We sat in silence, my eyes and mind still full of flames.

Palgi died within a month after I finished work and left the valley to travel in the hills. On our last visit, she spoke of her own

most days i find myself able to hold their pain with patience and mindfulness.

village, which was not far from where I would be traveling. We spoke of how clean the air and water are out of the valley, how cool the higher hills are during the summer-time. I remember sitting hand in hand, the skin taut over the long bones of her fingers, two rings, one of turquoise, one of coral, hanging loosely below the knuckles. She closed her eyes, felt the cool of that air, and the sweetness of that water.

Palgi. Bahadur. Padam. Bhim Kumar. Om Bahadur. Pokchi. Tilak Bahadur. Karmarenji. Man Kumari. Charlie. Bob. Freda. Tyler. Sitting, holding the death of each of these people, the frailty and transience of my own human shell has become more and more clear. Touching the weakened and broken skin of those like Palgi and Bahadur, who I believed were closer to death than I was or am, has unveiled my own fear and wavering acceptance of death. I do not believe that Nepalis fear death any more or less than Americans do. However, in the U.S. we have managed to distance ourselves from and sanitize the process and act of dying. Nepalis do not have this "luxury."

I witnessed Palgi's fear in the face of her own death. I watched people shrink away from touching her and others who were extremely ill. I found an ability to sit quietly with that fear. It became progressively clear that to move into work with death and dying in the U.S. would both challenge and support my Buddhist practice and the way I want to engage this life.

In this country and others, thousands of home-based hospice agencies mobilize resources into the homes of people dying with cancer, ALS, AIDS, dementia, pulmonary and other diseases, every single day. Families learn to be caregivers for their loved ones. Hospice staff provide support for families to address everything from pain management and bed sores to spiritual support, respite care and bathing, to funeral arrangements. The first door that opened to me in this field was in the area of grief and loss. Families and friends of those who have died find themselves staring into their own wounds, as I did at the time of Tyler's death. The scar of that loss, unique for each person, becomes an integral part of one's life. Slowly, each person learns how to heal the wound and weave strength and growth back into the tapestry of his or her life. I spend my days supporting people who are holding the severed strands of their own tapestry.

Most days I find myself able to hold their pain with patience and mindfulness. At the end of our dialogue, I am able to let go of their suffering, like blowing a soap bubble into the wind. On rare occasions, I find myself drawn into their wounds, the profound magnitude of the loss. Only a few weeks ago, toward the end of a lengthy bereavement phone call, I became restless, as if in need of air. I hung up and felt as if the entire core of my body had been transformed into dry, coarse sand. I was struck deeply by the magnitude of loss in this person's life. I sat on the floor right in the middle of that darkness and cried.

A lengthy bike ride and several hours later, the raw pain grew into a gift. In this work, I find it easy to settle into a sense that "I know." I examine a chart, read through the social-work assessment, and think that I might have some clue about how that wound feels for that individual. The reality is, I have no clue. That experience also reminded me how acrid grief can taste and renewed my ability to sit with that bitterness.

There are days when my meditation practice feels confined to a half hour of superficial breathing on a small black cushion. Thankfully, there are others days on which the same practice sustains my effort to sit as completely with the bitterness of pain as I do with the strength and joys of healing, with death as fully as I do with life.

A Small Step from the Lotus

Meggan Watterson

"ARE YOU LISTENING? Are you? I said get off...get the fuck off me...now!" Toby's words turn into a high-pitched scream as he pounds his head against the scratchy, gray carpet of the classroom's floor. I take a deep breath to steady my voice and repeat, "We're keeping you safe until you're able to count your quiet five." I scramble to find some other sentence or some other tone of voice that might calm him, but before I can, a loud slur of Toby's curse words force me to stay silent. I clamp my left hand tighter around his wrist as he struggles to pry his arm free. My right hand is pinning his shoulder down with a fistful of his T-shirt. I use this hand to block the spit he attempts to catapult over his shoulder. One of my legs is pressed into his thigh and the other is crossed over his calf to secure his foot.

This is not about me, I remind myself, this punch, this bite. This violence came far before either one of us and will outlive us both.

Another counselor is restraining Toby in the exact way on the opposite side of his body. We three have been in this position now for nearly half an hour. Unless he calms down in the next few minutes, we will have to begin the arduous and often dangerous struggle of escorting him into the treatment center's "Quiet Room," which is a euphemism for a small, locked, and padded space.

MEGGAN WATTERSON, 25, IS A DIVINITY SCHOOL STUDENT FOCUSING ON THE FEMININE DIVINE IN RELIGIONS AROUND THE WORLD.

Toby turns his neck as far as it will reach toward me and screams some vicious swear words. I can feel my face turning red. I can't hear his actual words anymore. I feel instead the horrific fear they communicate. This violence seems to be the only language he knows, as a nine-year-old, to express his pain and anger—which was the same violence that had been used on him at home. I can feel Toby's furious heart pulsing; I can see the shiny sweat on his face from his struggle to be free of me. But the real Toby seems far away, pulled inside to one of the many terrifying memories of being sexually abused. This is not about me, I remind myself, this punch, this bite. This violence came far before either one of us and will outlive us both. I try to remind myself of this as his wrist bends awkwardly to dig dirt-encrusted nails into my lower arm where he has been leaving his marks since I became his counselor. He's under my skin in this way.

At the beginning of Toby's intervention, the other children in the classroom were quickly led outside to an early recess. They walked around Toby, pinned to the floor, absorbed in their noisy back and forth about the new "hecka-cool" Nikes and about first dibs on the basketball court. This scene of two counselors holding down a frantic and terrified child is familiar to the kids—it happens every day at the residential treatment center. It's familiar to me, too. But today it's different. Usually I find some sort of skillful means to bring Toby back from his brutal memories to himself in the present moment. Sometimes I redirect him before his fear and anger even take hold by starting up our game of "remember when." He created it with me when I began as a counselor nine months earlier. As we were drawing quietly next to one another, he suddenly said, "Remember when I was a whale and you were a mermaid?" I responded with enthusiasm and vivid detail, and from then on, it was our own world we could escape into together. Eventually, this little ritual that enabled me to connect with Toby in a way that other counselors could not secretly led me to believe that I had something over my coworkers. Somehow I thought I was more selfless than they were, maybe even closer to the bodhisattva ideal that had inspired me to begin work with emotionally disturbed children.

The tips of Toby's sandy-colored hair are wet from his tears and matted to the side of his now puffy face. He turns toward me again, and I brace myself for the swear word or spit he will hit me with, but he just stares. And stares. The vacancy behind his eyes exhausts me. I wonder if this cycle of violence will ever end. His chest sporadically heaves from having emoted so much for so long. I worry he will begin to hyperventilate and just then he speaks. "You can't hold me down, not you, you're pretending you're not the same as me. Stop pretending!" His words hit me with a force

i walk slowly through the vestibule, hoping not to disturb the sanctity of the space with Toby's screams, which seem to be following me in a swarm around my head.

that stops my breath. I can't move…. I can't react…. I can only be with the heavy weight that is working its way through my body.

He had slapped me in the face a few days earlier. After processing with him and another counselor, I had imagined we'd been wearing monk's robes in that moment and that his slap was the essential step of ultimate awakening. I was humiliated by the physical slap, but it is his words that sting my face and awaken something in my core. I look down at my hand gripped around his wrist. My knuckles are white with strain. I slowly let my hand release his, and I begin to tremble. I feel weak. The other counselor watches me in disbelief and calls out for support staff in the adjoining classroom. I place my hands trustingly for a moment on Toby's back as he sinks with a sad and fatigued exhale into the ground. My supervisor emerges from the classroom next door in order to help the other counselor follow through with Toby's intervention. But he's completely silent and still beneath my hands. The three of us stare at his small frame for a moment together in silence.

Then, my supervisor and the other counselor lift him gently from the carpet as his shouts of protest return and quickly escort him into the Quiet Room. I can hear the children returning from recess clamoring down the hallway toward the classroom. I sit on the floor staring at my trembling hands. I ease myself up and take deep breaths to try to contain the swell of thoughts and emotions I feel crashing against my mind. The teacher enters the classroom with the children and walks quickly ahead of them toward me to tell me to leave for my lunch break. As I start toward the door, I feel the pain I had kept hidden for so many years finally break through to the surface. I feel ripped wide open and vulnerable.

I close the gate to the treatment center, cross the street, and walk toward Saint Cecilia's large wooden doors. The air inside the church is smooth and thick with the scent of candle wax. I breathe deeply. I walk slowly through the vestibule, hoping not to disturb the sanctity of the space with Toby's screams, which seem to be following me in a swarm around my head. Fortunately, the sanctuary is empty except for an elderly woman shrouded in layers of black lace. She lifts her head, bent above prayerful hands, and looks over toward me as I cross the expanse of wooden pews. I try to appear quiet and self-contained. I tuck my hair behind my ears and pull my sleeves down over the scratches. I feel obliged to explain my presence. But before I can speak, she smiles sincerely and motions me to sit. I find a seat with a clear view of Mary. Stained glass depictions of the New Testament reach out to either side of Mary with the words Our Lady of Perpetual Healing soldered into each frame. I stare at Mary's dove-white hands pressed to her heart and at the small tear affixed to her smooth cheek. I close my eyes and envision the bronze statue of Tara on my altar at home. I focus on her foot stepping out of the lotus petal and into the world. I think of the tear Tara emerged from and of her attribute of fierce compassion. Her chant begins to resonate through me as tears begin to slide down my own cheeks.

Out of the silence of meditation, Toby's accusation suddenly rings out: "You're pretending you're not the same as me." It pierces my heart, even just to hear it in my head. But here in the safety of the church, of Tara's image, I let myself open to the truth of his words. They rip into the illusion I had created that I was different from these kids. They take me back to why I have been able to connect with him and several of the other children at the treatment center. I know, like they do, that a child who has been sexually abused cannot decipher between a therapeutic

restrain and abusive restrain. I know that being held down regardless of
who or why incites the exact horror we are attempting to heal the children from experiencing. And the reason I can connect with Toby when
other counselors fumble for a way isn't because of some wise bodhisattva
shining from within me. It's because I know in my body their own suffering, their own tears of rage and grief. The line giving me power as a
counselor to being power-
less as a kid is much, much
thinner than I want to *He will never know the way he has*
acknowledge. When Toby *liberated me and changed the nature*
threw his work across the
classroom, knocked over *of my work as a counselor.*
his desk and ran for the hall
screaming he no longer
wanted to live, I was not just a concerned counselor—I was him. I look
down at my palms folded on top of each other as a resolution awakens
within me: I will never restrain a child again.

I imagine Toby sitting in the mauve-colored Quiet Room. I smile at
the faces I know he is making at the monitor who peeks in through the
door's little window to determine when it's time to release the touch-
sensitive lock and allow him to return to class. I envision Tara rushing to
sit beside him, brushing his bangs back from his face and holding him in
a way that dispels the fear he has told me of so often. I realize that he will
never know the way he has liberated me and changed the nature of my
work as a counselor. He will never understand how his directness, meant
to hurt me, gave me an authentic way of stepping into this world from
the lotus with a fierce compassion. Then I pray, knowing we are the
same, with my hands pressed tight to my chest, that somehow the laws
of karma or the good in the universe see to it that this small bodhisattva
receives his share of beauty and love. I walk slowly back to the treatment
center, holding in my heart the light of the votive I had placed at Mary's
feet in honor of all the lessons I have yet to learn from these children I
vow to suffer and heal with.

part three: livelihood

JUVENILE HALL DHARMA

Soren Gordhamer

I STARTED MEDITATION PRACTICE as a teenager growing up in a small town in West Texas—bored, confused, and suffering. I had a hunch that there was more to life. My father, a psychologist with an interest in Buddhism, left books outside my door in an attempt to help me. They were usually on spiritual practice or sex, two of the most difficult subjects for parents and teens to discuss. My father never took us to church growing up, and this was odd in the highly Christian town. As a kid I got chided for being an "anti-Christian," and a few parents wouldn't let their children play with us because of our lack of faith. Spirituality was always confusing for me. If we were not Christian, what were we, for crying out loud? We had to be something, hadn't we?

If we were not christian, what were we, for crying out loud? we had to be something, hadn't we?

My father passed along to me some tapes on Buddhist meditation during my teens. They stayed on my shelf for a number of months before I listened to them. In them, I found something that I had been looking for: an acknowledgment of the suffering I felt and saw in life. I then started practicing meditation on a somewhat regular basis. I was a

SOREN GORDHAMER, 32, IS CO-FOUNDER OF THE LINEAGE PROJECT, A NONPROFIT ORGANIZATION DEDICATED TO TEACHING MEDITATION AND YOGA TO INCARCERATED, INNER-CITY TEENAGERS. HE DIRECTS THE LINEAGE PROJECT'S PROGRAMS IN NEW YORK CITY.

"bathroom" meditator, rolling up a pillow and sitting in my parents' back bathroom because there was a lock on the door. I didn't want my siblings to know what I was doing, or my father to find out that I was actually taking his advice. These tapes became my refuge during my teen years, and I spent many evenings with their profound words.

> I wondered why more effort was not being made to introduce teens to meditation.

I then came to like the idea of being a Buddhist meditator—so much so that when, as a teenager, I came across the book *Zen Mind, Beginner's Mind*, I refused to read it. Having previously read a number of books on Zen, I certainly was no "beginner"! The practice was still mainly in my mind, not my heart. I got more involved with Buddhist meditation as I got older—going on retreats, traveling to Asia, sustaining a practice. About four years ago, I noticed how few young people were involved in the Buddhist meditation scene. I wondered why more effort was not being made to introduce teens to meditation. I then hooked up with the Spirit Rock Meditation Center Family Program, which had just started offering meditation classes for teens. While doing that work, I began to wonder if the practice could be useful to other, more at-risk populations of teens. A few friends who were practicing meditators had been incarcerated as teenagers, and we started to explore the possibility of doing this work with incarcerated teens in the local juvenile hall. It stuck; I've been teaching in juvenile halls and youth prisons for about four years, currently working at juvenile halls in New York City. These facilities are located in the poorest sections of the Bronx, Brooklyn, and Harlem.

Over these last four years, the teens have taught me a great deal about how to work with them. The biggest change is that I've gone from introducing meditation as something strange and foreign to something that they already know and do. "What is the difference between 'chilling' and meditation?" I sometimes ask. "What does it feel like when you are in the flow during a basketball game?" I explain that we all do some form of meditation already, and that in our class we will simply do it with more intention. This creates a different feel for the class, with less separation between experiences in their lives and meditation practice.

I had various motivations in beginning this work. One was my own experience as a teen and how much the practice helped me. Another was the need to get more young people involved in Buddhism. The third reason was that I wanted a real challenge. I thought, if this meditation stuff really works, shouldn't it be helpful to a larger population? If it's only useful for the primarily middle-aged, well-off people who come to my sitting group, then something is off. A friend who teaches martial arts says that there is a time in martial arts students' development when they wonder whether what they are learning will really work in a fight. The students go "looking for a fight." Going to teach meditation in juvenile hall was, in some ways, my way of "looking for a fight." I wanted to work with a population that did not know any of the usual rap, for whom the phrase "the Buddha said" meant absolutely nothing. There were no safe comments or phrases to hold onto; it had to be brought down to the basics. This, to me, was extremely exciting and frightening.

> if this meditation stuff really works, shouldn't it be helpful to a larger population?

Even though I'm the "teacher," I learn a great deal from incarcerated teens. Sometimes I feel like they are changing me more than I am changing them. They're always expanding my levels of patience, humor, and skillfulness. Many times, of course, I completely fall on my face. The class ends up in a fight, or they just look down and completely ignore me. But at the best of moments, they learn something and so do I. Here's one class where I really "got it": one of those moments where everything had the possibility to shift, if I could have the spaciousness and humor to let it.

_____

I walk into the youth division at Riker's Island in New York City for the third week of my classes. Riker's is one of the largest city jails in the country with about 16,000 inmates. It also qualifies as the largest youth jail in the country, with a couple thousand sixteen- to eighteen-year-olds. The entire facility is on an island in the East River, covered with massive fences and acres of barbed wire. To get to the facility where I work, I pass through five checkpoints, a bridge, and six locked metal doors. It takes about forty-five minutes to get from the front gate to the classroom. The teens here are being held for everything from truancy to murder. I offer my classes as part of their school curriculum during the day.

My first class is very difficult. It's a large class of about twenty-five youth. A number of them are interested in the class, but the ones who aren't refuse to be quiet. The teacher has left the room, and it is just me and the guys. I struggle to do my best, but I can't get control of the group. I sit down and have a discussion with three kids who seem to be more engaged. I keep looking around waiting for the teacher to come back, but he never does.

I'm happy to leave and walk to my second class, which does have a teacher present. As I begin, a large young man comes barreling through the door. "The king is here," he announces, banging his chest. He then gives a two-minute nonstop monologue that I cannot quite follow, but the gist of which seems to be the repeated assertion of his leadership on the unit. He walks over to me.

"Who you?" he shouts.

I tell him my name. He lets me know that he goes by LJ.

"Whatchou doin' in my class?" he asks.

I give him the short version of my usual rap. He shows mild interest. I get him and the ten others to pull their chairs in a circle. I begin by talking about how various people use meditation, and that even basketball teams like the Lakers do it to help them get "in the zone" or "in the flow" during games.

"What's it like to be 'in the zone'?" I ask.

LJ responds, "You do what you need to do without worrying about it." I ask him to say more.

"It's like when I was selling lots of drugs and making mad money. If I ever got afraid during a deal, if I wasn't paying attention, it would go bad. If I was confident, then it always worked out. I never worried, so it always worked out."

Many kids like him know about the power of the mind to affect certain situations, but they have rarely been shown how it can be used in more positive ways. Following up on one of his comments, I add, "But it did not always work out because here you are."

"Not for selling drugs. No one caught me at that!" he says, smiling.

"So what did you get caught for?" I ask, knowing that I was treading into unknown waters.

He leans back in his chair and looks at me.

"Body," he responds, implying that he had killed someone.

I have no idea if he is serious or just playing his role as tough guy on the unit. I decide to go back to our earlier discussion.

"So how did you feel when you were doing a deal?" I inquire.

"You felt alive, right? Part of the excitement was that you had to be alert and watchful during a deal. We are all looking for the feeling of being alive, and sometimes it is only through dangerous activities that we know how to do that. When there is danger, we have to be attentive, but maybe there is another way to that attentiveness. Today we will explore other ways to that place." His interest increases a notch.

We do a short meditation, which goes extremely well. Everyone is very focused. A number of the kids briefly open their eyes to see if LJ is doing it and immediately close their eyes again once they see him sitting silently. When I ring the Tibetan bells to end the meditation, a number of the kids smile in approval. Afterward, we talk about their life at the facility. After our class, they go back to their unit, have about an hour of recreation time, then have nothing planned after that. They usually play cards or watch TV. I ask, "Why aren't there any programs like this in the evenings?"

LJ, who seems to speak for the group, responds, "People are too scared to be working with us. How many people want to come at night to a unit of fifty convicted guys? Nobody." He has a point, but I also know that some of it is a lack of program funding. We pay twenty to thirty grand each kid per year to imprison these youth who will soon be back on the streets, but cities across the country provide little to no funds for programs to help them make any kind of positive change.

we are all looking for the feeling of being alive, and sometimes it is only through dangerous activities that we know how to do that.

As I leave this class and walk through the hallway to my next one, I hear a shout from down the hall, "Yoga-man." I look up to see a familiar face. It's a kid named Chris who was in my class a few weeks ago.

"Why didn't you come to my class today?" he inquires.

I tell him that I just go where they tell me.

"Hurry up," Chris says. "Come this way to my class, just for a few minutes."

As we walk, he says to me, "You got the bells with you?" I nod. We walk quickly to his room. It feels like we are sneaking off to the bathroom to smoke a joint. I follow him into a room of eight kids and no teacher. He gathers them up. "Yo, check this out. We're going to do a meditation. Everybody chill and listen to him." I'm a little nervous and in a hurry, afraid the teacher might come in and catch us. I tell them to close their eyes for the meditation. Chris breaks in. "They gotta sit up straight first." He models the appropriate posture. I tell them to sit up. We do a short meditation and end just as the teacher is coming into the classroom. She grins as she sees her class sitting in a circle looking very calm.

Recently I have found that though I go in to teach meditation and yoga, what matters more than anything is the spirit of the work. Much of it seems to be developing a particular trust in the group. Last week, I was leading a class that had been quite difficult in the previous sessions.

what matters more than anything is the spirit of the work.

The kids were unsure what I was doing at their facility, and there was a palpable tension in the room. There is often a certain degree of posturing that happens before trust develops. During the yoga, a muscular guy with various tattoos, who looked like a cross between a street fighter and Taoist sage, asked me, "Yoga-man, can this stretch help me get bigger muscles?"

I looked at him seriously and said, "Actually, if you do this enough, you could get huge muscles like me." He looked at me curiously, scanning my scrawny frame. I could almost hear his thoughts: "Does this homey really think he has big muscles?" No longer able to keep a straight face, I let out the hint of a smile. A wide grin spread across his face. Laughter rippled throughout the class. The spirit of the class had changed.

DO ANDROIDS DREAM OF ELECTRIC DHARMA?

Josh Krieger

IN THE SPRING OF 1992, having just graduated college and begun a full-time job as a computer programmer, I found myself still feeling awkward inside my adult body. Maybe as a child I'd read too much science fiction, watched too many Nova episodes, or seen Star Trek one too many times, but I secretly expected my high-tech training to transport the adult me to a new body, a new place—somewhere special. Oddly enough, I never expected to find myself alone in a windowless office cubicle staring at a computer screen all day.

It was during this time, shortly after I had begun to explore Zen practice, that I met Tod, a new co-worker about my age. One day Tod arrived at work sporting a pair of large, dark black, slip-on sunglasses—the kind my grandfather wore over his prescription glasses. In the right lens was a roughly hewn rectangular hole in which was mounted a small cube-shaped computer screen. The screen was connected to a portable computer strapped to his belt, and the computer was in turn connected

> Tod began to tell me how he believed that the next phase of human social transformation would involve the conflation of human and computer intelligence—a machine/human symbiosis.

JOSH KRIEGER, 30, IS A ZEN STUDENT AND A COMPUTER PROGRAMMER WHO SPECIALIZES IN WRITING SOFTWARE FOR PEOPLE WITH DISABILITIES. YOU CAN VISIT HIS WEBSITE AT WWW.ZAFU.COM.

to a bizarre device with about ten small buttons in parallel lines. Smiling at the contraption, I asked Tod about it. He showed me the computer and the miniature screen, which I tried on over my own glasses. The device with the buttons was a one-handed keyboard where individual letters were typed as if spelling out chords on the frets of a guitar. As I wore the whole contraption, Tod began to tell me how he believed that the next phase of human social transformation would involve the con-

I had been listening to Tod with the growing sense that I was a visitor at a freak show.

flation of human and computer intelligence—a machine/human symbiosis. With the primitive technology that I was now wearing, we were at the beginning of that age. There I stood, wearing these magic glasses. I could see Tod through my left eye while superimposed on his image was a computer screen projected onto my right eye. I felt like the cyborg played by Arnold Schwarzenegger in the movie *Terminator*—the terminator who went back in time to destroy a human resistance in the past so that computers would control the world in the future. I took off the glasses.

Tod told me that as he spoke to people while wearing the computer he would often type in things that they had said and maybe add a few ideas of his own. All these notes he would quickly file in a database that augmented his natural memory. Multitasking in this way, he could keep a real-time record of his mind and the minds of others. Through a cellular modem he could access anyone throughout the world.

"Why do you want to merge yourself with the machine in this way?" I asked Tod. "Why this kind of symbiosis?" He sat up straight, smiled, and said that if he went away somewhere, or if he were to die, all his ideas had been recorded, mirrored within the database that he carried around with him. They could then easily be transferred to another individual or looked up in the future as a record—a kind of black-box flight recorder salvaged from the pieces of a wrecked airplane. Grimacing, I said, "Don't you think your identity, your self, is bigger than just the thoughts and ideas you have? Doesn't it, at the very least, include your body and feelings?" He replied confidently, "The body is a sack of pain."

Throughout the interchange I had been listening to Tod with the growing sense that I was a visitor at a freak show. Standing there looking down at him seated in his chair, I watched a misshapen man struggle for my amusement. But now our roles switched. He was watching me with amusement and I was a caged visitor—a signifier of humanity's primitive past, powerless against a quickly changing world.

Each year, in daily life and on meditation retreats, this story keeps returning to me. At first I used it secretly as a way of praising myself, the guy who is aware and practices dharma, and putting down Tod, the guy who is lost in technological fantasies of immortality and control. Recently though, as science fiction has moved closer to science fact, I have been appreciating this recurring story as one part of my life-*koan* of how I can fully embrace the modern world as a manifestation of the Buddha's inexpressible radiance. I can't help but recognize my love and fascination with computers; the way, like Tod, the computer manages to extend my mind and body to reach around the world, to communicate with people and find information anywhere, anytime. But I must also recognize the negative side to these virtual experiences of connection—feelings of disembodiment that have often led me to practice Zen meditation as an antidote to high-tech delirium. It has required an intense effort to negotiate a middle way that neither involves becoming a Luddite nor unquestioningly embracing the latest high-tech gadget.

somehow though, whether it's surfing the world wide web or writing software for work, the moment the screen lights up and i begin to dialogue with the computer, i find myself quietly disappearing into an ethereal unity of man and machine.

I have tried to direct my mindfulness practice to the actual experience of what it's like to use my computer. Somehow though, whether it's surfing the world wide web or writing software for work, the moment the screen lights up and I begin to dialogue with the computer, I find myself quietly disappearing into an ethereal unity of man and machine. Pains and hungers vanish. I'm only vaguely aware of the seat on which I am sitting, the room around me, and strangely, a body that feels like it contains me. As I stand up after a particularly engaging session at the computer, often hours have passed. I feel a bit disconcerted and disconnected, almost like I am wrapped in a thin sheet of gauze, lightly constricted in movement and sight. If Dogen Zenji were alive today, would he choose to talk about "dropping off body and mind," forgetting oneself in the activity of using the computer?

Fearful of these disassociative experiences, I have sometimes found myself fleeing into meditation retreats vowing that I would never touch a computer again. But here I am; here we all are, continually in relationship with each other through these fantastically relational machines that have become an integral part of our modern world. These days my work as a computer programmer writing software for people with disabilities often brings me into contact with people who are deaf, blind, or physically disabled. For many people with disabilities, a portable or wearable computer has already become an integral part of their bodies—a lifeline that helps them travel and communicate, to more fully participate in a world that is already unfriendly to their disabilities. A friend who is blind has a speech synthesizer that reads web pages to him. Suddenly he is able to listen to newspapers, books, meet new people, and apply for jobs, things that he could never have imagined before. Another friend, a writer who can't type because of repetitive stress injury, is now able to write again because of speech recognition software for her computer. I often wonder where the body ends and the technology begins, to what extent the machine/human symbiosis is already an integral part of our lives.

One night after work, I find myself at the Zen center that I frequent. Finally there's the chance to be silent, to disconnect, if only for a moment, from the fast pace of modern technology. I sit up straight and attempt to live a posture, breathe a whole body. After all these years of practice, it still isn't easy for me. I silently struggle to sit still, to occupy, as Tod called it, this "sack of pain." As if in retribution for my attempts to establish peace of mind, intense feelings surge forth: anger, joy, lust, and sadness. I have to go to the bathroom. I'm hungry, my legs hurt. I begin thinking of endless places on the Net to surf and of software that needs to be written. Anchoring my awareness in the rising and falling of my belly, my meditation practice seems to be able to contain this tale of sound and fury. I feel more connected to my body, closer to the people sitting near me, and alive with the zendo's creaking wooden floors. At a time when an internet-year lasts only three months, there is something ancient and primal about this experience. I feel the animal alive inside of me. How could virtual fantasies of control and machine/human symbiosis compare to this?

As if in retribution for my attempts to establish peace of mind, intense feelings surge forth.

A bell rings, signaling the end of sitting meditation, and it's time to let these experiences go even as I try to grasp at their fleeting aliveness. For a moment, I'm reminded of the romantic and entirely anachronistic Zen saying, "Chop wood, carry water." It's the twenty-first century and my everyday activity has nothing to do with chopping wood. Now it is simply "Work on the computer, go to meditation." I am engaged in a living cycle of work and practice that includes the modern world.

Freeing Tibet, Freeing Myself

Adrienne Stauffer

I WAS INTRODUCED to both Buddhism and Tibet when I was sixteen, the summer that I was doing organic geochemical research at Indiana University in a program for high school students. I had flirted a little bit with Eastern philosophy before, but overall I hadn't given much thought to how that philosophy could be integrated into my life. But my inattentiveness to all that changed in one moment. I was walking down the street after a bad day, and a man in a parked minivan poked his head out the window and said, "Smile, cheer up." I humored him a little, blew him off, and started to walk away. As I was walking away, he shouted "Free Tibet!" I turned around and asked, "How do you know about Tibet?" He asked me the same question.

I told him that a dear friend in my research program had told me about her friend Julie's involvement in the planning of the first Tibetan Freedom Concert, in San Francisco. At that time, whoever Julie was and whatever she was doing had gone in one ear and out the other, because I didn't know much about the situation of Tibet except that it needed to be freed. I couldn't even point to it on a map. When I mentioned Julie, the minivan full of strangers all exclaimed, "We know Julie!"

These six strangers had driven from New York to Indiana to see the Dalai Lama speak the next day. They needed a place to stay and asked me to help them out. I tried to find a friend in town for them to stay with because my research program didn't even allow me to have female friends

ADRIENNE STAUFFER, 20, IS A STUDENT AND AN ACTIVE MEMBER IN THE ORGANIZATION STUDENTS FOR A FREE TIBET.

over, let alone six male total strangers. I had no luck finding the friend, so I hid these six New Yorkers in my tiny dorm room that night.

We spent the entire night talking about Tibet and the Chinese occupation that has cost so many human lives. They told me about atrocities, such as forced sterilization and abortion, rape, imprisonment, and torture of even monks and nuns.

i didn't know much about the situation of Tibet except that it needed to be freed.

They also told me about the oppression of Buddhism and the lack of freedom that Tibetans must suffer in their own country. These descriptions shocked me, first because of their content, and second because I, who considered myself a socially aware and informed individual, had no idea that this was happening. If I had no idea, how many other people in the world didn't know? And why didn't they know? That night, I decided that I would educate myself as much as possible about the situation in Tibet and then educate others to the best of my ability. I was outraged and disgusted that human beings could treat each other in such a way, but I didn't know how to harness my feelings about it to form useful actions.

The next day I saw His Holiness speak. I sat in the fifth row between the driver of the minivan, who is now a dear friend of mine, and a Tibetan monk. Seeing His Holiness speak was an incredible experience. After hearing about the horrible events going on in his country, I could not comprehend how this exiled leader could be so loving and compassionate toward the very people who were destroying his land. Not only was he glowing throughout the entire speech, but the entire auditorium full of people was resonating with an energy that I couldn't even describe. This man's presence made me want to become like him, to be able to be so happy in the face of despair, and to love my enemies unconditionally. How did he do it? I wanted to discover the secret to his infinite kindness.

After that summer, I became heavily involved with the organization Students for a Free Tibet (SFT) and learned more about political activism than I had imagined possible. Now I am so deeply engrossed in the Tibet situation that I can hardly remember what life was like before this activism discovered me. After educating myself about the situation in Tibet, I began talking to people at my high school about what was happening. The topic mostly came up in history classes when we were discussing China. I would typically go on some tirade about how the Chinese government was oppressing people and their religion, committing genocide, destroying the environment, and quickly eliminating an entire culture. After a year of heated debates with students and teachers, I had learned how to intellectually defend my point, but I hadn't gotten far in terms of controlling my anger about the situation. It became clear to me that I was not reaching people with such an attitude, nor did my anger do anything to benefit the cause. After realizing that my methods of action were ineffective, I reminded myself of the Dalai Lama's calm, peaceful manner and how it had touched me so deeply. I began to talk to people about Tibet in a different way and noticed that people were more willing to listen to me when I focused on compassion and nonviolence.

When I went to college, I continued to focus on the nonviolent aspects of the Tibetan movement when talking to people. My work sparked the interest of two of my friends, and we three decided to start a chapter at the University of Chicago. Because there were no other SFT chapters in Chicago at the time, and because it's a large city, we had a lot of work ahead of us. We made sure our presence was known on campus through tabling, passing out flyers, and planning both cultural and political events. We became involved with the Tibetan community in Chicago by supporting their events and inviting them to participate in our activities. We also began communicating with other SFT chapters in the Midwest and planned demonstrations and conferences in Chicago. Although our chapter is now well-established, I still have frustrating encounters with people who are not willing to listen, do not believe that the Chinese government has killed over one million people in Tibet, or simply do not care about the cause. When I become frustrated with these experiences, I think about the Dalai Lama, a simple Tibetan monk, who has been faced with the destruction of his nation and people. I remind myself that my frustrations are nothing compared to those of this man, who must constantly deal with powerful people who are not willing to do their part to put a stop to the endangerment of his own people. I continue to be inspired by the sense of peacefulness that I could feel in his presence, even when he was talking about the violence that has plagued his country.

Through my involvement with the political movement, I have learned about the culture, religion, and lifestyle of the people that I am trying to help. It has also led me to study Buddhism more in depth. I took a Tibetan Religion class and learned about the way that Buddhism transformed Tibetan culture. I also began to learn the Tibetan language, and through translating religious works from Tibetan to English, I learned more about the beliefs and practices of Tibetan Buddhists. In addition to the practical reasons for exploring my interests, Buddhism seemed to be everywhere around me.

i am more effective as an activist when i employ my Buddhist beliefs.

As my involvement with Students for a Free Tibet continues to grow, and as I continue to explore my own spirituality, I see that I am more effective as an activist when I employ my Buddhist beliefs. I can reach more people when I control my anger about the situation in Tibet by both emphasizing and demonstrating the compassion of the movement. It is unfortunate that it was the struggle of a peaceful country that brought Buddhism to my attention, but at the same time I am grateful that I was presented with the opportunity to learn about myself through political activism and Buddhism.

A Flash of Lightning: Inner Revolution and Social Transformation

Diane Biray Gregorio

In 1988, I took a semester off from my sophomore year at the University of Pennsylvania to live and study in the Philippines, the country of my birth. As a typical eighteen-year-old from the suburbs of America, who had not lived in the Philippines since I was a baby, I was completely unprepared for the shocking images of poverty and injustice that I encountered on the streets of Manila. I lived in a tiny apartment with thirteen relatives, slowly realizing the daily struggles of living in a country where the vast majority of people live below the poverty line. The experience utterly transformed me, personally and politically; I returned to the States a very different person. The life plans I harbored before—to become a millionaire by age twenty-five—seemed less relevant, not to mention self-centered. I felt a passionate responsibility to use my education to address the injustices I had witnessed.

By my senior year, I was saddled with heavy student loans. Many of my classmates were heading toward Wall Street investment banking or management consulting with one rallying cry: "Show me the money!" Yet the memories of my time in the Philippines rang in my conscience. After much soul-searching, I decided to try out the corporate world for a few years in order to pay back some debts, save a little money, and then, I promised myself, I would work in the nonprofit sector. With my

DIANE BIRAY GREGORIO, 29, INSPIRED BY THAI FOREST TRADITION OF THERAVADAN BUDDHISM AND THE TIBETAN BUDDHIST TEACHINGS OF HIS HOLINESS THE DALAI LAMA, CO-FOUNDED THE BOSTON CHAPTER OF THE BUDDHIST ALLIANCE FOR SOCIAL ENGAGEMENT (BASE) AND IS A PH.D. STUDENT IN SOCIOLOGY AND ORGANIZATIONAL BEHAVIOR.

diploma, a brand new, navy-blue business suit, and my first briefcase in hand, I ventured into the wilds of Corporate America.

I was making an obscene amount of money for a twenty-year-old. I worked insane hours: over twelve hours a day, six days a week. To balance the pressures of work, I got caught up in a pattern of living large, partying wildly, and spending carelessly in the few hours I wasn't in the office. In spite of fervent attempts to numb myself with work, play, and consumption, I could not erase the fact that I had become profoundly unhappy. I felt as though my soul was drying up inside, disconnected from a sense of deeper purpose.

The life plans I harbored before—to become a millionaire by age twenty-five—seemed less relevant, not to mention self-centered.

In order to reconnect with the inspiration I felt upon returning from the Philippines, I started volunteering for Oxfam America, an international development organization committed to long-lasting solutions to hunger and poverty. I felt an immediate charge from contributing to what I really cared about: greater equity and justice in the world. Eventually, I realized that I had to make some drastic changes in my life in order to be true to the sense of purpose that was reawakening within me.

Although I realize that it is possible to live a life of wisdom and compassion in whatever profession—whether a CEO, lawyer, car mechanic, or an activist—during that stage of my life I needed to shift my course dramatically in order to feel alive again. I quit my corporate job and took a position at Oxfam for half my former salary. I began to confront my unhealthy patterns of spending and partying. I broke up with a boyfriend that I had been with for nearly three years. I started training in martial arts, became a vegetarian, and tried to teach myself how to meditate. I also came out as bisexual. Fittingly enough, it was during this time of living in a more authentic way that I discovered Buddhist teachings.

Anushka was my first dharma friend. She had just returned from a two-year spiritual journey in Asia—doing meditation retreats, visiting monasteries and ashrams. She was a bona fide dharma bum. Here was someone to whom I could relate. She wasn't some sort of distant sage, an old man in a long robe and a scraggly beard, sitting on top of a mountain. She was a woman of color, a lesbian about my age, who was deeply committed to the spiritual path. She too had been raised Catholic. I liked her outlook on life, her joyful demeanor, and the way she carried herself with calmness and positive energy.

During that stage of my life I needed to shift my course dramatically in order to feel alive again.

Through this friendship, I began seriously practicing meditation at the Cambridge Insight Meditation Center, and later at Insight Meditation Society and Abhayagiri Buddhist Monastery. Devouring the dharma through as many retreats, classes, sittings, and books I could get my hands on, I felt I had finally found my spiritual home. I began to experience firsthand the natural reservoir of peace, clarity, compassion, and wisdom that resided within me.

My work at Oxfam was also taking on a spiritual dimension. As my heart and mind were opening to the suffering within me, I also began to open to the vast suffering across the world. Over the course of five years, my job took me to twenty-five countries in Asia, Africa, and Latin America, as well as to poverty-stricken parts of the United States. I marched with women demanding their human rights in Northern India. I visited an indigenous Mayan village in Guatemala struggling against the exploitation of the coffee industry. I met with a black community reclaiming its land in post-apartheid South Africa. I trekked to a refugee community in the mountains of the Philippines, living on desolate land ravaged by deforestation. I worked with small family farmers struggling to survive in the heartland of the United States.

Yet, no matter where I was on the globe, the same questions weighed on me. Why is it that in spite of endless efforts we still live in a world where nearly 1.6 billion people live below the poverty line? Why does the gap between rich and poor continue to grow? How is it that the oppressed sometimes turn around to become the oppressors? Why are those of us in wealthy countries unwilling to face how our own patterns of consumption, corporate domination, and weapons production contribute to these problems? I began to suspect that social, economic, and political change were not enough to remedy these intractable problems. The root of these ills was much deeper.

Ironically, new insights into these questions began closer to home, in a cabin in Maine during a snowy retreat, December 1994. I had brought along a copy of *A Flash of Lightning in the Dark of Night*, His Holiness the Dalai Lama's commentaries on the Mahayana classic *A Guide to the Bodhisattva's Way of Life*, by Shantideva. True to the title, the beauty and truth of these teachings struck me like a bolt of lightning, straight into the core of my being. Embodied in the ideal of the bodhisattva—a being who realizes buddhahood not just for her own peace and freedom but for the benefit of all beings—I saw for the first time the connection between my spiritual practice and my work in the world. It slowly dawned on me that, although I was treating them as separate, these areas were one and the same. They both sprung from the same source—the yearning to understand suffering and experience freedom —whether in myself or in the world. It was that New Year's Eve, sitting on a riverbank blanketed by the hush of falling snow, that I knew from the depths of my being that I could never turn back.

> I began to suspect that social, economic, and political change were not enough to remedy these intractable problems. The root of these ills was much deeper.

Shantideva's exquisite passages and the lucid wisdom of His Holiness's commentary reverberated throughout my life. Indeed, over time, I found that my work and my practice fed each other in a mutually reinforcing cycle of awareness. The more I saw suffering in the world, the more I was inspired to understand suffering in myself. The more I understood suffering in myself, the more I could begin to understand it in others. The more peace and clarity that flowed from this understanding, the more I could offer in service. In the ongoing dance of dharma practice and social action, it became clearer that what I had suspected was true—social, economic, and political struggle *alone* would not be enough. These teachings sparked in me the firm belief that, in order to strike at the true roots of poverty and injustice, we need a radical inner transformation of the greed, hatred, and delusion that resides in our own hearts and minds as individuals and as a society. The introduction to His Holiness's book, *Essential Teachings*, explains this clearly:

> None of the major terrible problems that threaten survival of the earth can be solved by merely institutional or political methods. *Humankind to survive has to undergo a massive and unprecedented change of heart, an ordered and passionate spiritual revolution that changes forever our relation to each other and to nature.* It is only from such a revolution that the new vision the planet so desperately needs can arise—a vision that sees the connections between every thought and every action, the relations between the obsession with the individual self and its hunger for false securities and every kind of exploitation that is ruining the world.

While there is no turning back, there are endless questions. I continually ask myself, "What form does my service need to take right now—meditation retreat or social justice activism?" So far the answer to this life-*koan* has involved taking the time for each at different points, but also experimenting with the integration of dharma practice with social justice work. I completed an internship with Dr. Jon Kabat-Zinn's program on Mindfulness-Based Stress Reduction (MBSR), working in an inner-city clinic that teaches meditation and yoga to a diverse population including people struggling with addictions and homelessness. I started an MBSR program at Oxfam, engaging my colleagues on an exploration of mindfulness in the workplace and in our work for social justice. I launched a chapter of the Buddhist Alliance for Social Engagement (BASE) in Boston. With my partner, Robin, I am about to introduce meditation and yoga to an after-school program and to a cooperative working with low-income immigrant women. I maintain a daily meditation practice and set aside time for longer retreats. I try to live a life of simplicity and mindfulness and act in accordance with Buddhist ethical precepts—a formidable task in the midst of a busy urban life. My challenge is to continually remind myself that inner revolution and outer revolution must go hand in hand. As Mahatma Gandhi implores us, "We must be the change we seek."

Although I feel a strong draw to a simple life in a forest monastery, I have chosen to go back to graduate school, pursuing a Ph.D. in Sociology and Organizational Behavior. Entering the academy may seem an odd choice for someone committed to social change. Yet it is not difficult to see that when debating the great social issues of our day—whether it is poverty, drug abuse, or violence in the schools—we often attempt to solve the problem using the same logic that got us there in the first place. Is there a fresh perspective that can offer us a more penetrating explanation of why things are as they are, one that cuts to the source? Like all the great wisdom traditions, Buddhism points to the possibility of being free from the cycle of unenlightened existence. It is my hope that I might add, in some small way, to the growing chorus of voices who are demonstrating the power of a dharma lens to uncover the underlying truths at play in contemporary social problems. Perhaps this might help in the creation of solutions that address the origin of social ills where they actually lie—at the center of the human heart. Following humbly in the spirit of the great teachers and socially engaged Buddhists before me, I hope somehow to contribute to an emerging culture of awakening.

> I try to live a life of simplicity
> —a formidable task in the
> midst of a busy urban life

SOCIALLY ENGAGED BUDDHISM INSIDE-OUT

Diana Winston

W E'VE HEARD THE STORY of the dharma in its travels across the Asian continent, how at each stop it blended and mixed with the culture at hand. We've heard that within each country the dharma then emerged as a unique expression of the individual. Look at Tibetan and Thai Buddhism—although related in underlying beliefs, they are now far distant cousins in form. And so it is in each of us; as the dharma enters our bodies and minds, it gets mapped in new and unique ways, merging with our inner landscapes. It blends and swirls into what is already inside; it falls into cracks and excavates and chips away. And ultimately our personal geography becomes so entirely fused with the dharma that the end product is a melded terrain where the features are uniquely our own.

The dharma, when it traveled to and through my body, came face-to-face from the beginning with a political activist. I was drawn to Dharamsala, India, not for the spiritual teachings of His Holiness the Dalai Lama and the community in exile, but because an activist friend told me (and this was 1989) that the Tibetan cause would be the up-and-coming human right's issue. She promised she would never forgive me if I didn't use a few of my hard-earned organizing skills to help in the autonomy movement. Although only 22 at the time, I had been an activist from the cradle. Neo-liberal Jewish-intellectual-*cum*-hippy parents had instilled in

DIANA WINSTON, 33, A WRITER, ACTIVIST, AND TEACHER OF MEDITATION (ESPECIALLY TO TEENS), IS THE FOUNDER OF THE BUDDHIST ALLIANCE FOR SOCIAL ENGAGEMENT (BASE) PROGRAM AND SERVES AS ASSOCIATE DIRECTOR OF BUDDHIST PEACE FELLOWSHIP IN BERKELEY, CALIFORNIA.

me a strong ethical conscience and an inalienable sense of justice. I grew up a mini-feminist, raised on *Ms.* magazine. I lived in collective households and marched for nuclear disarmament on my own volition at thirteen. In college my activism grew more tactically and theoretically sophisticated. I attended multiple radical political theory classes, organized for women's rights, sat-in against apartheid. There were a host of campaigns that marked the anger-fueled college activism in the late '80s—in spite of, of course, Reagan's insistence that economic security was the cure-all for my generation.

ultimately our personal geography becomes so entirely fused with the dharma that the end product is a melded terrain where the features are uniquely our own.

I saw myself as way too political to be spiritual. So my months in Dharamsala, earnestly educating Westerners about the plight of the Tibetans, took an odd turn when a vague tugging below my conscious awareness drew me in the direction of a meditation retreat. I went, despite my seemingly better judgment and Marxist programming. Ten years later I can only bow to the mysterious workings of karma. A few teachings of the Buddha and I was hooked. There was more to life than I imagined after all. I spent the next two months in intensive retreat and felt the teachings flow into and change me. I was awestruck at their beauty; though highly cynical, I was powerless to do anything other than absorb.

When I met His Holiness the Dalai Lama a few weeks into my retreat (back in the days before his fame rivaled rock stars' and you could actually visit with him), I carefully constructed a question. I wanted to know (of course) about the relationship between dharma practice and social change work. His screeners found it too political—they were careful then about what the Chinese might think at any turn—and watered down the translation to: "Can you be involved in service work and still meditate?" Sitting in a cramped room with my fellow spiritual aspirants, fame-struck by this bodhisattva incarnate, I awaited his reply. His Holiness, with his characteristic ability to cut through all nonsense, locked eyes with me and replied, "Dharma is service." Those three words have stayed with me since as a guide and a source of ongoing reinterpretation and reflection. As the dharma spreads into deeper, more hidden and unknown places in my body, those three words have been my torchlight.

"what about the world? what about the world?" it was my body speaking.

I soon became a *vipassana* practitioner when a fellow dharma bum/traveler mentioned free retreats in a monastery in the south of Thailand. I packed my backpack, headed for the beach, and took a nosedive into Theravada Buddhism, which almost immediately became my primary practice. The following years were spent in long retreats of several months in the West, deepening my intuitive assimilation of the dharma. I was teaching my mind, step-by-baby-step, how not to cling, and my reward was periodic glimpses of the peace of a free mind. True to form, throughout this five-year period I asked my Western teachers with unfailing regularity, "But what about worldly suffering? How does what we're doing on the cushion translate out? How could it make a difference to injustice, poverty, racism, consumerism...?" The answers I received were never terribly satisfactory. They didn't have the depth I was craving.

To pay for my retreat life I had taken a series of odd and depressing jobs, from waitressing at a sushi bar to secretary work to the nadir of all jobs, telemarketing. The dharma insights on retreat in between the jobs were compelling and kept me going. But at 26 I began to ask myself, "What next? Go on retreat and work to pay for retreat; not a bad life, but what about the world? What about the world?" It was my body speaking.

I was sitting in a cubicle in a fluorescent-lit office next to fifty other cubicles all exactly alike. I was in Phoenix, Arizona, possibly mentioned in the Pali canon under Buddhist hell realms, especially in the summer. I was sweating in spite of the air-conditioning. Depressed, lonely, my mouth chattered on automatic pilot to the unsuspecting customer on the other end of the phone line, "Hi, I'm calling from Dial America, Golden

Press, and Sesame Street Books, how are you today?" Beneath me the dharma was churning through bodily streams and rivers of thought and experience flavored with the despair and confusion of how to live my life; the *dukkha* of the unanswerable questions assaulted me. Suddenly, out of nowhere, an underground spring gushed—social action, service, dharma practice, community. Yes, yes, put it altogether... "And how old is your child?" Of course the world needs this, we need to figure out how to bring activism and dharma together, and the only way to do it is to try. An idea is born. "Great, cuz I'm sending you a free sample just for taking a look at our offer...."

Together we created a socially engaged Buddhist community.

I sent a proposal to the Buddhist Peace Fellowship, which landed, as karma would have it, on the desk of a woman who had also been dreaming of something like this. And so I was ultimately hired first to research and then to design and create the Buddhist Alliance for Social Engagement (BASE) program.

Initially a group of ten of us participated in BASE. We were all given service or social action positions of 10-30 hours per week, directly engaging with people who were suffering through hospitals, homeless shelters, or inner-city schools; or working to change oppressive structures through activist organizations like antinuclear groups. We met twice weekly to meditate, study, support each other, and discuss the interface of dharma and social action. We met monthly for retreat days. Together we created a socially engaged Buddhist community.

BASE began as an experiment. We had few answers about the merging of the spiritual and political; we knew we wanted instead to provide a container to explore the questions. And from the beginning we realized we had hit on a need within the Buddhist and activist communities: the fusion of Western social-change wisdom—tools and techniques, theory and praxis of participatory decision making, feminism, group process, Marxism, analysis—with Eastern dharma wisdom—tools and techniques, theory and practice for cultivating the compassionate heart, under-standing interdependence, selflessness, and so on.

Since 1995 more than fifteen groups have sprung up across the coun-try, primarily in the Bay Area, but also in Boston, Tennessee, and Col-orado. Some BASE programs have offered dharma wisdom to those whose primary work was in social-change fields; some have introduced Buddhists to service and activism. Some grew up around a particular type of work: Educator's BASE, Prison BASE, Homelessness BASE. BASE continues to grow, and its discoveries feed the growing movement of socially engaged Buddhism in the West.

The lessons have been innumerable. We've learned the importance of an integrative practice, one that connects inner, personal work with outer, social transformation. We've seen that the greed, hatred, and delu-sion that exist in our own minds is no different from what's outside in society and the structures within it. We've seen the falseness of the sep-aration: dharma is service. Personal and social suffering can't be sepa-rated. As a group we have supported each other with our dharma wisdom when burnout seemed imminent. We've pushed, inquired, and sent each other into deeper levels of commitment as practitioners of meditation and of social change. We sit together in community, our fundamental practice: learning to develop the state of presence that can stay free amidst all the horrors and degradations in this time on this planet. We get angry together, argue, dis-cuss, encourage, play, gossip, meditate, cook, and sing. We plot the dharma rev-olution.

we had few answers about the merging of the spiritual and political; we knew we wanted instead to provide a container to explore the questions.

We comfort the one who has broken up with her lover, and the one who's furious over sweatshop labor. We squirm in our discomfort when it seems that we can't do anything right at all. We recognize our humanness and our failings, and we celebrate our victories as bodhisattvas-to-be. The journey is much more interesting with others along. Our political bodies merge with our Buddhist sensibilities. We come out whole.

Now back to my body. Those years coordinating the BASE program fed the hunger, facilitated the fusion, the merging of my geography with the ever-permeable dharma. Ironically it led to deeper dharma practice, a year as a Buddhist nun in a monastery in Burma, a koan-like choice that confused the hell out of me. Here my political beliefs collided with my spiritual longings. Would my presence in Burma in any way legitimize the military dictatorship? But could I give up my compulsion to practice with my spiritual teacher in the land of its origin? This one caused me to sweat, both from the political/spiritual dilemma and from the unbearable Burmese permanent-summer weather. From the hard work of noting every single moment, I sprung back to my social explorations. I spent another half year working with socially engaged Buddhist movements across Asia. I taught meditation at a Buddhist school to preteen rural village children in India. I met with Asian activists who had set the stage for the Western socially engaged dharma, including Dr. Ariyaratne, the founder of Sarvodaya, the world's first Buddhist-based development organization.

Currently I've returned to the states, to Buddhist Peace Fellowship (BPF) and to continued practice in socially engaged dharma. At last the integration feels more natural, a part of me rather than pieces I have been trying to paste together. I now identify as a Buddhist-activist rather than as one or the other. At rallies I march under the BPF banner and remind my fellow activists not to demonize the CEO of Monsanto and to take a breath when they're red in the face. In my dharma center I share the socially engaged dharma, reminding my sangha members that the meditative practice and the world out there don't make strange bed-

> I share the socially engaged dharma, reminding my sangha members that the meditative practice and the world out there don't make strange bedfellows.

fellows. I fly to Seattle to protest globalization. I sit at home on my cushion each day. I write and think about and feel inside how it all becomes one dharma.

The merging is not complete by any means. My inner landscape is at times marred by confusion and contradictions: Is that rally giving me half the benefit of a day of retreat? Is liberation from samsara more important than ending poverty? How can I waste my time in the monastery when the world is aflame? Lately the questions seem less dualistic and more answerable with, "Well, it's all under construction. I learn through the doing." The dharma mixes within my body, moving inside me, marrying and unmarrying, smoothing edges and discovering new crevices yet uncharted, until finally the new self-terrain appears with features of socially engaged Buddhism's unfolding in the West.

part four
REFLECTIONS

Reflections

O NE BOOK that had a deep impact on me is *Pure Heart, Enlightened Mind*, the diary of a twenty-something American-Irish woman who joined an all-male Zen monastery in Japan. Leaving Boston in the late '70s, Maura Soshin O'Halloran did a thousand days of Zen training that required such austerities as never sleeping lying down. She outstripped the Japanese monks so thoroughly that the roshi declared her his eventual successor. I wept when I read that she died in a bus accident in Bangkok in 1982, just after her enlightenment was confirmed. The precious gift she left me was to see Buddhism through her eyes, the eyes of someone like me. The nitty-gritty of *zendo* politics, culture clashes, gender issues, modernity, and changing relationship with her mother profoundly shifted my conceptions of Buddhism to a subtler, more complex and also challenging place.

All things eastern were clumped together with all things occult in one aisle of the health food store.

Likewise, in compiling and reading the narratives in this book, I found myself again challenged to question many assumptions. Yet certain aspects of these candid writings resonated with and shed light on reflections I had, for example, regarding teachers and authority, the American culture, and religious pluralism. Thus, the closing section of this book consists of three threads: observations about young Buddhists based on my last three years of experiences and the writings in the book; discussion of the issues arising from those observations; and probing questions and ideas that I feel are important for young Buddhists to begin thinking about. Some of the discussion covers issues only alluded to in contributors' writings.

My intention is not to provide a definitive sociological analysis of the emerging generation of Buddhists but simply to begin an examination of some of the issues raised by this generation. By no means are the topics I've chosen complete.

As I am a young Buddhist myself, I do not feel especially qualified to provide answers to questions that are raised. In this time of tremendous personal growth, I find that my own views turn inside out as I gain more experience in the world and study Buddhism in the academy. At the same time, there are certain things from my own life and experience with this book that I feel strongly should be discussed. It is my hope that the speculations in this section will stimulate and provoke broader discussion as our path in Buddhism unfolds.

Zen and Now

Imagine that thirty years ago only a handful of people did meditation and the ones who did were considered radicals. No one had heard of the Dalai Lama of Tibet. All things Eastern were clumped together with all things occult in one aisle of the health food store, which smelled exotic and was run by someone who'd just started making their own tofu. Three decades ago, such things were considered so unconventional that they were called "counterculture" and even "un-American."

The context within which young Buddhists are exploring dharma today is notably different. The Dalai Lama draws a crowd of thousands to Central Park; yoga is in every women's magazine; bookstores have significant sections dedicated to Buddhist books put out by major publishing houses; "power beads" are a huge moneymaker. These things are a part of so many American's lives that what was counterculture then is simply alternative today.

Young people choosing a Buddhist path today are exploring a now-thriving path that lies within the circumference of what is generally acceptable. While taking a step on the Buddhist path may feel radical in many ways, it is no longer necessarily seen that way by the culture at large. The young people of this generation have considerable luxury in choosing their spiritual path and don't necessarily have to spend much time justifying those choices to those around them. In fact, Buddhism among young people is actually seen as very cool!

Becoming Buddhist

When I mention Buddhism in casual contexts, often heads turn. The conversation begins to buzz with questions and stories about Richard Gere, meditation retreats, and recent books. Young people are turned on by Buddhism. Hearing mentions of Buddhism through the news, rock concerts, movies, and magazines serves as a spark that kindles an eagerness to absorb more about this unusual and time-honored religion. How do those young Americans who were not raised in Buddhist homes come to earnestly study and practice in the Buddhist tradition, some even becoming self-identified Buddhists?

Often the link to Buddhism comes not from grand revelations but from simple, accessible things: seeing a colored sand mandala in the local museum painted by Tibetan monks, picking up a book on world religions, listening to temple chanting on a CD, or buying a Buddha statue. Or perhaps a young person may have a Buddhist friend, parent, or relative, or find enjoyment in the meditation at the end of a yoga class. Young people often describe that initial contact as "*this* is it," or "I've come home." That immediate attraction becomes the basis for further inquiry and learning.

Young people of this generation have considerable luxury in choosing their spiritual path.

As the exploration of the Buddhist path unfolds, young people reflect back on their earlier childhood religious experiences. Many young Buddhists come from families that strongly emphasized a particular religion. Questions raised in church or the synagogue were formative in stirring the spiritual pot: Who is God? What is freedom? How do I actually put into practice what I'm taught? Young people who turn to Buddhism report that liturgy, catechism, and sermons were not sufficiently addressing these metaphysical and everyday questions, and that the institution was too restricted, hierarchical, or dogmatic. Rather than throwing out religion altogether, these young people explore alternatives. Buddhism seems to fulfill several needs. For some, it elucidates a deeper meaning and appreciation for a home tradition. Others like Buddhism's pragmatic approach to ethics and the utility of meditation for finding inner peace but feel it's important to integrate Buddhism with the culture of their home tradition that has been important to their identity.

Young people often describe that initial contact as "this is it," or "I've come home."

Other young Buddhists come from families that had no religion at home. Very often, these are children of Baby-Boom parents who themselves may have rejected or felt detached from their family's faiths. In these cases, it seems that it is the lack of religion that initiates a deep questioning. These young Buddhists say that it was the missing something, the spiritual vacuum, that pushed them toward Buddhism.

Whether from dissatisfaction with a previous faith tradition or in the search for spiritual meaningfulness, the draw of Buddhism on young people today is strong enough that a significant number begin to seriously commit to developing a Buddhist path as a focal point in their lives. Interestingly, even with a clear decision to cultivate the Buddhist path—and a life of retreats, dharma talks, commitment to sangha, travel to Asia, extensive reading, daily ritual, meditation, and prayer—many young people are reluctant to formally identify themselves as Buddhist—even some of this book's contributors! There are diverse reasons why these young Buddhists avoid saying, "I am Buddhist."

Among those from strongly religious backgrounds, frequently Christian or Jewish, many carry forward an aversion toward things seeming to smack of institution, hierarchy, dogma, or unquestioned authority. These young Buddhists can be reluctant to align themselves with any institution or doctrine. Many find Buddhism attractive because it seems to offer the possibility of a spiritual life without association to "institutional" religion.

In addition, those from other religious backgrounds don't always make a full conversion to Buddhism but weave that other religion together with Buddhism to one degree or another. As well, young people might incorporate elements from other faith traditions into their Buddhism. In some cases, enough people are doing this to garner a new hyphenated label, such as Jew-Bu or UU-Bu (Unitarian Universalist). But for others, what label accurately points to the combination of their religious practices?

Another significant reason young Buddhists tend to avoid saying, "I am Buddhist" is based on philosophical grounds: some believe that applying any label to themselves reifies a sense of self that conflicts with the Buddhist doctrine of no-self.

Young people find creative ways to get around this problem. For example, the most common answer among young people in response to "What religion are you?" is "I *practice* Buddhism" or "I am a Buddhist *practitioner*." This emphasis on practice seems

It was the missing something, the spiritual vacuum, that pushed them toward Buddhism.

to allow a compromise between avoiding full identification with Buddhism while still conveying that Buddhism is a big part of one's life. Another reservation young people have is that they don't feel they have the authority to claim they are Buddhist without some kind of official recognition. Many Buddhist centers don't have initiation ceremonies or rites of passage. Those that do often require long-term commitment to a teacher and sangha that young people naturally have not had much time to develop a relationship with. Given this, young people are perhaps justifiably reluctant to announce themselves as Buddhist. The aspect of formal initiation may explain why young convert Buddhists affiliating with, for example, Nichiren and Tibetan Buddhism, which have more ritual structures, are more likely to identify themselves as Buddhist. Those in the West affiliating with Zen and vipassana/Theravada, which tend to focus more on meditation, are less certain about their claim to Buddhism.

Although no young Buddhists I know have brought this up, I speculate that one reason rests on a subtle aspect of Buddhism's position in the West. From a cultural perspective, calling oneself "Buddhist" is ambiguous in the American context. Here, all the Buddhist traditions now live side-by-side, colliding and mingling vigorously. To say one is "Buddhist" might mean any number of things: a *sumi-e* painter, a vipassana meditator, a student of Daisaku Ikeda, a yogi, an advocate in Students for a Free Tibet, and so on. The few young people who will say they are Buddhist are often quick to qualify the statement with which sect, sangha, and teachers they predominantly associate. Furthermore, though Buddhism may be acceptable to broader American society, it is often not well understood; misperceptions may be one reason that young people avoid stating their Buddhism to a non-Buddhist. Some people think that Buddhism is a justification of a free-wheeling morality or lifestyle, a reason for psychedelics, a severe discipline, or that it's New Age and cultish. These are outdated ideas, but they persist nevertheless in popular conception. On the other end of the spectrum of preconception is that a Buddhist does not swear, get angry, eat meat, have nonmarital sex, or throw a good party. Altogether, these misperceptions could be preventing young people from identifying themselves with Buddhism publicly.

Young people, often already occupied with the question "Who am I?" are finding the question of a Buddhist identity a challenge, touching on wide-ranging issues of allergy to institution and doctrine, of philosophical grounds, of syncretism, initiation, and the American perceptions of Buddhism. As this generation grows up, it will be interesting to see whether the answer to "What religion are you?" becomes more straight-forward or more complex.

The Dharma Deli and the Spiritual Supermarket

For young people beginning to explore Buddhism, the differences in appearance, practice, and doctrines of things called "Buddhist" can be bewildering. Even the essays in this book present diverse individual expressions of the dharma. How does a mystical vision of Tara square with meditation as a kind of psychotherapy? How does the desire to escape the mundane world of family as a monastic relate to plunging into the hub-bub of New York City and finding inner still-ness? Is chanting the title of the Lotus Sutra commensurate with marathon-running as a spiritual discipline? How have young people approached the diversity of Buddhisms in America?

Young people say that at first this diversity leads them to comparison shop: Which tradi-tion is most authentic, most efficacious, most pure? Or, young Buddhists try to reduce the diversity down to a common denominator: "Buddhism is about nirvana" or "All these traditions are really metaphor-ically talking about the Pure Land." However, increasingly exclusivism and reductionism in reaction to the problem of plurality are being seen as imperfect solutions for the kind of society young people encounter today. Perhaps then it is helpful to think not of "Buddhism" but "Bud-dhisms." Rather than becoming disappointed in not finding the most authentic Buddhism, it may be better to open to the abundance of Bud-dhist traditions. These different perspectives from the Buddhisms of America may provide rich and creative solutions in ways that homoge-nizing, reducing, or discounting Buddhisms cannot.

At the same time that young people peruse the "dharma deli," there is the question of the spiritual supermarket. One of the amazing things

Young Buddhists can be averse to aligning themselves with any institution or doctrine.

about America is the opportunity to mingle and converse with many faith traditions, especially the Christian and Jewish, though increasingly the Hindu, Sikh, and Muslim. Young Buddhists, especially those coming from other faith traditions, often discuss how to relate to the plurality of religions around them. To what extent can other religions' wisdom be drawn upon? Is it meaningful to engage in interfaith dialogue and practice? How do we weigh that against the advantages of committing to one tradition alone?

on the other end of the spectrum of preconception is that a Buddhist does not swear, get angry, eat meat, have nonmarital sex, or throw a good party.

The essays in this book reflect the problem young spiritual seekers face today of the abundance of teachings from many religions. Is it possible to be a Buddhist-Christian, believing in ideas of no-self and rebirth at the same time as soul and heaven? When it comes to prayer, is one praying to God, Krishna, Avalokiteshvara, the Buddha, Allah, or Jesus? Within Buddhism itself, is it possible to be someone who studies both Theravada and Tibetan traditions, which employ different meditation techniques and have different cosmological emphases?

Some young people seem to navigate these diverse religions in creative ways that address their contemporary needs. Someone may do zazen to clear the mind, Gita chanting for devotion, ashtanga yoga for mind-body fitness, and go to church on Sundays with her Christian family. Others find that the problem with creating a pastiche of practices, whether inter-religious or inter-Buddhist, is that it's hard to find community support, to be the student of multiple teachers, and to evaluate one's spiritual progress. As this generation continues to grow in its exploration of the dharma deli and spiritual supermarket, we will need to continue talking about this balance of grounding ourselves in one tradition while also being open to new ways of doing things.

Generational Dialogue

As a young Buddhist myself, I wondered whether there were any particular considerations to being young when beginning in Buddhism. I asked older Buddhists about their own youth and their perspectives on it in hindsight. One reminded me that even in the Buddha's day, a person's age was a consideration for admittance into the sangha. Several passages in the *Vinaya* discuss issues around age. For example, in one passage the Buddha allows full ordination only for those age twenty or older. Novices younger than twenty would need their parents' permission. The contemporary situation is similar in some ways. Many teenagers upon first hearing the dharma have wanted to throw off the yoke of the world and dash full-on toward enlightenment—either by taking an intensive retreat or by joining a monastic or lay practice community—only to be asked by teachers and parents to give the decision some time. At the same time, teachers recognize that this energy and enthusiasm can be useful when starting the path.

There are other advantages to being young. On the one hand, young people are generally in good health and may have fewer physical impediments to the rigors of intensive meditation, chanting, or bowing. On the other hand, young people may believe they're immortal because of this natural health and thus lose sight of one of the strongest motivations to delve into Buddhism: clarifying the matters of sickness, old age, and death. Older Buddhists reflect that that kind of denial of mortality can take the preciousness out of every living moment fully. At the same time, young people are seen as having fewer preconceptions that get in the way of seeing what's actually happening. One college professor said that working with young students in meditation was refreshing because they had such open minds, curiosity, and sincerity.

How does the desire to escape the mundane world relate to plunging into the hubbub of New York City?

Yet young people can be very goal-oriented. Youth is, after all, a time of setting goals. So, with that modus operandi already in place, it's not surprising to see young people thinking they'll become enlightened before they're thirty! Sometimes that kind of goal-orientation can obstruct a present-moment experience and letting go, says one dharma teacher. On the other hand, despite goal-orientation, some young people have the kind of flexibility in the structure of their lives that many older adults do not and thus are more able to explore and take risks—as some of the stories in this book so clearly illustrate.

Yet, because of the lack of life experience, young people tend to see things as all-or-nothing, easily leading to an achievement-or-failure mentality, as well as to unforgiving judgments of self and other. A teacher is all right or all wrong, practice means one thing and not the other, only one kind of dharma is orthodox—these ways of thinking tend to change through life experience.

It seems that the challenge facing young Buddhists is to temper these youthful strains by relying on the wisdom of older Buddhists for guidance while harnessing the advantages of being young. One tremendous resource in the older generation that many young Buddhists can tap into is their parents. For example, most of the young people in this book and elsewhere have benefited from parents who were Buddhist or experimented with Buddhism. Parents have been mentors, role models, and teachers for many of their children: having family morning meditation, introducing books, visiting the temple. In this regard, the emerging generation of Buddhists is fortunate to have the approval, guidance and support from a generation of our parents.

Of course, not every young, aspiring Buddhist has full approval or even any approval from their parents. Many are uncertain of how their parents, who may be of a different tradition, will react. In some cases, young people have misjudged their parents, assuming they would be angry, only to find them surprisingly supportive. In other cases, young people have gotten reactions of betrayal and disappointment from religious family members. In these cases, the internet—email, chat rooms, discussion boards—seems to be playing an increasingly important role in providing community support for young people who are not on settled religious terms with their parents.

At the same time, young people have also been a conduit of dharma back to their parents. Some parents have become interested in learning more about Buddhism because of their children. One older friend of mine had been involved in Buddhism for decades, and his mother, at the age of eighty, began doing retreats when he introduced dharma to her. She's in her nineties now, which just goes to show, it's never too late to start! More surprisingly, a few parents have even returned to Buddhism, which they explored in their own youth, as their children have become more interested in it.

Because of this kind of intergenerational flow, we should not be misled into thinking there's a huge generation gap. The purpose of this book is not to set off young Buddhists from the previous generation, characterizing the emerging generation as especially distinctive, cooler, or an "improved" version of the older Buddhists. However, the younger generation does have a significantly different set of memories and cultural references. None of us remember the '60s, or what it was like to grow up without Buddhism being around. Few of us remember the scarring scandals in Buddhist communities of the late '70s and '80s or had to make the wrenching decision to emigrate in the wake of war. Yet while the emerging generation may feel distinctive in some way, we are much more continuous with the older Buddhists as we rest upon the dharma seeds they've sowed in the last thirty years. Additionally, as older and younger Buddhists have a good thirty to forty years of growing and learning together ahead, there is more a *generation non-gap*. Thus, young Buddhists should be wary of becoming a go-it-alone generation. Rather, young Buddhists can continue to learn from and honor the previous generation while challenging our generation to be aware of itself as it develops along the path.

someone may do zazen and go to church on sundays with her christian family.

Another advantage of being a young Buddhist today is that the West now has a remarkable resource of skilled Buddhist teachers and leaders.

The challenge facing young Buddhists is to temper these youthful strains while harnessing the advantages of being young.

A generation ago, young people had to have the drive, leisure, and finances to go to Asia to get this kind of instruction. Today, not only do many skilled teachers from Asia make this their home, but a generation of Western teachers has also come to maturity.

Growing up in the dharma scene, I've witnessed a generation struggle with how to treat the matter of teachers. Out of suspicion of authority, some took a do-it-yourself approach that had disastrous results. Others were part of communes where the teacher demanded absolute submission, unquestioned authority, as well as money, labor, and sometimes even sexual favors. Some gurus disempowered students and became like parent figures. In short, the older generation has experienced difficulties in both going solo and in losing critical distance in an overly reliant teacher-disciple relationship.

Although difficult to quantify, it appears that a good proportion of young Buddhists today, especially beginners, opt for not having teachers, mentors, or even community at all. Some are reluctant to be drawn back into anything resembling bad experiences of hierarchy and authority from childhood faith traditions. Others have been drawn to Buddhism precisely because they think it doesn't require anything from the outside. A common belief about Zen, for example, is that all one has to do is sit on a cushion in the privacy of one's home in order to make spiritual progress. Yet in traditional Zen a *roshi* is considered integral as a corrective lens to meditation practice. In my view, it is critical for young Buddhists to draw upon the hard-learned lessons of those before us by first establishing some kind of relationship with other, more experienced Buddhists and then considering the balance of trust and confidence in a teacher coupled with good judgment and independent evaluation.

In view of the older Buddhists' experiences, there are two other potential imbalances young people can make regarding a teacher. First, Americans can be extreme in according too much faith in Asian teachers simply because they are exotic. We've tended to project an idealized image onto Asian teachers and can be disappointed when we find they're also human. On the other hand, sometimes we don't give enough credit to non-Asian teachers and become overly critical or irreverent toward them. Second, young people are inclined to search for The Great Master, longing to study with the so-called powerhouses of Buddhism. They seem to overlook people in their own backyard who have years of experience but who may not consider themselves teachers. When relating to teachers and leaders, young Buddhists might consider the offerings of Asian and Western teachers and of local instruction.

Born Buddhist

America now has a substantial group of young people who were born and raised as Buddhists, coming from the many Asian immigrants after 1965 and the non-Asian, older Buddhist families. Although these young people often have very different stories to tell, there are many shared experiences.

The most strongly identifiable characteristic is the role of parents, dharma teachers, monastics, ministers, abbots, priests, lamas, preceptors, mentors, and friends. Young Buddhists report that these

> young people have also been a conduit of dharma back to their parents.

elders were all pivotal to both the introduction and understanding of the Buddhist path. The significance of such relationships in their lives possibly hints that Buddhism cannot wholly be understood through books and self-instruction alone. As can often be read in the essays of this book, it seems that some of the deepest lessons are learned through the direct relationship to an experienced, elder Buddhist.

Those who grew up with Buddhism reflect on wonderful memories that have added richness to their present-day experiences. A bow to the

> young people are inclined to search for the great master— they seem to overlook people in their own backyard.

floor is not just a bow but a reminder of the time when one learned it from a monk, a reenactment of thousands of other bows, a way of honoring other altars at which one bowed before over the years. Other memories are often of the lovely, magical understanding of Buddhism in the eyes of a child. The fairy tales of Buddhism, the bodhisattvas floating around, images of the Pure Land, the magnetic smile of a *geshe*: kids grow up not intellectually knowing about Buddhism but feeling it artistically, emotionally, and imaginatively. Sometimes Buddhism can seem dry to those who come later in life because that component of imagination and mystery is missing. Art, drama, storytelling, and music have not been of much concern to convert Buddhists in America, though this is changing. Perhaps young Buddhists can consider expanding this side of Buddhism as adults; it's downright fun and a very human way of relating to religion.

At the same time, born-and-raised Buddhists, while enjoying mythical realms as children, find that they must make a deliberate effort to examine the Buddhist teachings intellectually upon entering adulthood. The many lessons from parents and teachers are only partly understood in childhood, and it isn't until later in life that all those seemingly incoherent teachings come together to form a valuable framework. For example, at some point, a young adult might ask what it really means to practice the bodhisattva path and will return to the texts she saw her mentors studying. As some child-Buddhists fall away from Buddhism when they become adults, it seems that this intellectual component seems critical for sustaining the dharma into the adult years. Very often, the decision to understand "that thing my parents did" comes on the heels of a real crisis—the death of a parent, a brother's paralysis, a reckless life of drugs, a car accident—much in the same way that many convert Buddhists come to the dharma. In this sense, and in the sense of a critical intellectual component to Buddhist practice and doctrine, those raised with Buddhism and who remain Buddhists as adults are not so different from those who convert.

This intellectual aspect of Buddhism brings out another problem for born-and-raised Buddhists. While those who've grown up with dharma feel at ease with things that normally perplex beginners, we are sometimes disadvantaged by assumptions formed from knowing something simply because it's always been there. We can be surprised by the "obvious" questions beginners ask that perhaps we ourselves could have asked in the first place, such as, if there's no self, what gets reborn?

Culturally, those young Buddhists raised in non-Asian Buddhist worlds have felt alienated from the rest of society that didn't expect to see, for example, a white kid meditating like the Buddha during grade-school recess. Thirty years ago, since Buddhism wasn't nearly as accepted as it is today, those of us who were kids had to struggle with the misunderstanding and puzzlement of our middle-class American friends. Sometimes, because we could also stand outside our Buddhist communities, those communities themselves looked very strange. It wasn't always easy to integrate two very different worldviews. In this way, these non-Asian Buddhists have had a similar challenge of biculturalism to that of Asian Buddhists living in America. However, possibly that bicultural quality also gives us some freedom to stand outside either culture and offer critical reflection.

Kids grow up not intellectually knowing about Buddhism but feeling it artistically, emotionally, and imaginatively.

It's significant to note that the "Asian" experience of Buddhism, in many ways, is not all that different from the non-Asian. Non-Asian Americans tend to think that they couldn't relate to the "ethnic" experience of Buddhism. The narratives of the Life Stories section reveal that there is far more in common than not.

Of course, whether one comes to Buddhist practice early or late in life is not as relevant as how it's lived from then on. However, those who choose to remain Buddhist from a childhood of Buddhism may have a place within young Buddhism at large. They carry the memories of what did and didn't work for the generation before; the challenge of appropriateness with teachers, for example. Or these young Buddhists can pass on the skillful discernment's garnered over time, such as the finer distinctions between detachment and nonattachment, and rebirth versus reincarnation. And perhaps this population of Buddhists can help newcomers feel at ease that Buddhism, beyond the Asian lands, has a home here in the West.

Life Choices

For some young people, being Buddhist means reorienting one's entire life direction around the dharma. A surprising number of young Buddhists show enthusiasm for taking up the monastic path. Whether this is an effect of an initial "falling in love" with Buddhism, a dissatisfaction with prospects as a rent-payer and office worker, a way to free up resources for a life dedicated to service with others, or a way to go straight to the ultimate goal of enlightenment varies from person to person.

Contemporary young monastics report that they encountered a number of obstacles in seeking ordination. The lack of a strongly established and extensive Buddhist culture in the West may make this path difficult to pursue, or even clearly define. When a young person expresses the desire to pursue the monastic path, it is often the case that parents, friends, or even fellow Buddhists, are not always supportive of this radical choice. How does one convince a mother that it's better to give it all up than to give her grandchildren to dote over? How can one persuade a father that spiritual success can outmatch professional gains? Although this is often a challenge, there are also some parents who have shown tremendous support of their children's unconventional choice, becoming patrons, attending the temple of their children, or even taking ordination themselves.

Sometimes when people think of monks or nuns, they think of someone high up in the mountains, in a remote monastery or a cave, trying to escape the world through enlightenment. Although there are some monastics that pursue isolation, for the most part, monasticism is a highly engaged communal activity that sends many monks and nuns into the thick of the world. Young monastics, like those before them, are debating how to engage such ministry, which seems so worldly, while pursuing the path of renunciation or retreat meditation. Interestingly, young lay Buddhists entertain the same debate, especially those who take a socially engaged path: What is the balance of retreat and inner cultivation with that of activism?

> we can be surprised by the "obvious" questions beginners ask that perhaps we ourselves could have asked.

It is extraordinary that a young person today who has unparalleled access to any lifestyle would relinquish romance, career, a good coif, and blue jeans in favor of asceticism, service, shaved head, and robes. In what ways can the American sangha support such aspiring monastics? Likewise how can we sustain those monasticlike lay people who want periods of intensive practice away from the routine of the world?

While some young Buddhists orient their lives around monasticism, others ask themselves how Buddhism can integrate into their longer professional career plans. As young Buddhists move into the work world, they must ask themselves the same question other young people ask: "In what direction should I turn my career?" Often this question stems from studying one of the arms of the Noble Eightfold Path, Right Livelihood.

What vocations are fulfilling of a life in the dharma? Young people seem to be answering this question in three ways. One is to bring lessons from the dharma into a job that might not be related to Buddhism, such as computer programming or teaching in the public schools. A second way is to pursue jobs that are more explicitly Buddhist, such as teaching meditation, being a Buddhist Studies professor, or running a temple or center. Sometimes the impetus to pursue employment in the dharma can come from a kind of idealism that the only way to practice Right Livelihood is this way, or that Buddhist jobs will be less stressful or require less training. However, a number of bright-eyed Buddhists are surprised to find that the dream job in their ideal dharma center was as demanding as anything in the "real" world.

The third way that young people today are energetically taking on Right Livelihood is through social engagement, which marries the dharma with activism. Socially engaged Buddhism is a fascinating development in contemporary Buddhism. It advocates that sitting on a cushion is not enough: one must take the fruits of practice into the world and work for social justice, environmental change, and world peace. It seems many young adults are focused on grassroots activism, seeing inner transformation as a foundation to engaged Buddhism and not as an end in itself. These are no shrinking-violet Buddhists, but people who wholeheartedly seek ways to bring their dharma work to some larger benefit. It is sometimes surprising to meet such energetic young people who are not the self-absorbed, superficial kids the media groans about. Perhaps there will be a growth of socially engaged Buddhism in this generation following upon the seeds of sensitivity sown by those of the world-peace '60s.

Buddhism and Pop Culture

After forty years of tremendous growth and change of Buddhism in America, Buddhists are beginning to step back to assess what's happened and where Buddhism is heading. Web-zine and magazine articles as well as entire books are increasingly addressing the role of American society in Buddhism and vice versa. Young Buddhists, who will begin to become part of this dialogue, need to be aware of these issues. Already, young Buddhists are expressing their thoughts on a wide range of subjects regarding the American culture. Of special interest, however, are the topics of material culture and the media's effects on Buddhism.

MATERIALISM

Regarding the prevalence of material culture, young Buddhists are not in agreement about whether the increasing presence of Buddhism in boutiques is beneficial. Consider, for example, the trend of wearing "power beads"; some young Buddhists feel that the bracelets lead people to ask deeper questions, noticing that the Dalai Lama not only wears one but also thumbs it constantly. Others feel that once again a religious tool is being marketed for mass consumption, watering down a profound part of Buddhism. This kind of marketing suggests that one can *buy* something spiritual instead of working for it.

Similarly, there is concern that Buddhism seems to be entering the larger society through the very vehicles of self-centeredness and materialism that Buddhism philosophically repudiates. Retreats can be expensive, and many of them are geared toward self-improvement. A quick flip through the back of any Buddhist magazine shows a preponderance of Buddhist items for sale, such as *zafus*, incense, bells, charms, audiotapes, clothing, and jewelry. This Buddhist materialism

> HOW does one convince a mother that it's better to give it all up than to give her grandchildren to dote over? HOW can one persuade a father that spiritual success can outmatch professional gains?

may not be bad. Some young people are drawn into Buddhism because of these aesthetic offerings. In fact, in Asian countries people flock to get talismans, trinkets, pamphlets, and things related to living saints, temples, holidays, and sites of miracles. It can be argued that physical objects are an important part of religion. The concern among young Buddhists then is whether this kind of materialism will take hold at the level of spiritual consumption. It can be easy to think, If only I had the right bell...*then* I would be able to really practice, and *then* I will really be Buddhist. In relating to the material culture of Buddhism, young people need to remember that we can't get Buddhism in a box. Meditation is hard work; compassion and service require perseverance; keeping ethical codes requires discipline.

The Media

There she was on the television screen: a tanned woman in her late twenties, her praying hands covered in henna tattoos, *mala* beads draped from her thumbs. She had a nose piercing, all-cotton Indian garb, bangles and multiple earrings, streaked blonde hair tied up casually, smiling peacefully at the camera. "Thousands of Buddhists and spiritual seekers gathered in Central Park today to hear the teachings of Nobel Peace Prize winner the Dalai Lama of Tibet," the CNN narrator glowed. I looked at the image in surprise—I had just been there. Of the forty thousand gathered on that cloudy, cool August day, this woman was an exception to the demographic. Sure, I saw one cross-dressed man who needed a shave, some lovely made-up Tibetans, and a few drugged-out people. But the majority I observed, including myself, were casually attired middle-class people sitting quietly with their backpacks and sneakers set to one side of a blanket.

The image revealed the disparity between what Buddhism in America actually is and what it appears to be in the media. Clearly, CNN had to comb the crowd to find a woman like that. Why would they choose her then? Is it because they think that to most Americans, Buddhism is a practice for only the most unconventional of citizens? Or is it that the image of this woman is much sexier to the imagination than me with my glasses and jeans? The media presents images in the form that they think most people will relate to. At the same time, it prescribes the way people will think about Buddhism. Media, even Buddhist media, not only meets preconceptions but also creates preconceptions.

A number of bright-eyed Buddhists are surprised to find that the dream job in their ideal dharma center was as demanding as anything in the "real" world.

In a way, Buddhism has become somewhat glamorous because of the media. Names bigger than ones we know in Buddhism are now attached

to it. There are fund-raisers and gala events with such star power that
some joke that Buddhism has gone from being the Middle Way to being
the Upper Middle Way. For young people interested in Buddhism, an
awareness of media-Buddhism is important. In some ways, the media
makes Buddhism more accessible to a large audience. But in other ways,
it prescribes the boundaries of
what's considered Buddhist, in effect
excluding some people from looking into it further if they think they
won't match it.

we can't get buddhism in a box.

Generally, young Buddhists have
expressed concerns that the media's appropriation of Buddhism dimin-
ishes the depth of dharma even as it makes it more accessible to mainstream America. There were mixed reactions to movies like *Little Buddha*
and *Seven Years in Tibet*, too, because although they spread a powerful
philosophy, they also sensationalized Buddhism. While commercials
flashing the saffron robes of Buddhist monks expose the public to their
beauty, such commercials are seen as trivializing the sacred.

Furthermore, regarding Buddhism, the seduction of the media can be
at cross-purposes with the Buddhist path. "Obey your thirst," as Sprite
advertises, means that we should be subordinate to our immediate desires.
"To be one with everything, you must have one of everything," a car ad
proposes, meaning that happiness is a result of acquisition. These messages are aimed at propelling a consumer culture of increasing desire and
satiating it. Buddhism, on the other hand, advocates reducing possessions
so as to reduce desire, and reducing desire to reduce attachment, the well-
spring of most suffering.

———

It's possible that Buddhism in the American pop culture of materialism
and the media is simply a contemporary expression of a fairly malleable
tradition. Interestingly, many young people have their first contact with
Buddhism through popularized dharma: receiving a Zen calendar, buying

a laughing Buddha statue, or seeing the character of Tina Turner chant *Nam-myoho-renge-kyo* in a movie about her life. Yet more prevalent among young Buddhists is a general anti–pop-culture attitude. Once on the path of cultivating dharma they tend to avoid things stripped of deeper meanings, like power beads from a store, in preference for more powerful symbols, like a mala bestowed at an initiation ceremony. Perhaps this antipop attitude stems from the fact that young people come to Buddhism because they want something outside of a mainstream that venerates pop culture: Buddhism has a very different message and can be a refuge. At the same time, Buddhism is becoming more absorbed into that same mainstream. That may be why so many young Buddhists feel ambivalent when they see the mainstream co-opting Buddhism in the media and in materialism.

some joke that buddhism has gone from being the middle way to being the upper-middle way.

The Orient Express

While young Buddhists in the West are making Buddhism more relevant to the American culture in which we live, many are flying over to Asia to deepen in dharma, just as the older Buddhists did. Most of the contributors to this book have spent extensive time in India, Sri Lanka, Burma, Thailand, Korea, Japan, China, and even Tibet. They go not to see the Taj Mahal or lay on the beach but to search deeply inside by practicing with traditional teachers and observing Buddhist cultures firsthand. The movement of travelers going to Asia is not a mere trickle of dreamers wanting to lose themselves in another world, but a flood of serious and down-to-earth young adults earnestly making a journey. Junior-year-abroad programs to study Buddhism for one or two college semesters are extremely popular!

Why are young people still going to Asia when, in fact, Buddhism has been pretty well transplanted to America? Not only is there access to the Buddhisms that the previous generation imported, but there are also countless temples in the Asian communities that have grown since mass immigration opened up in 1965. In other words, why do we keep looking over the fence when Buddhism is in our backyard?

One reason is that there is gratification from making a pilgrimage—a key aspect of religion—to the spot where it all began. Second, for non-Asian Buddhists especially, there is a feeling that the Buddhism in America is not "authentic." Some feel the need to affirm that we've got it right over here in the West. Others want to become absorbed in a fully Buddhist world, like Thailand, where there is a weight and dignity that comes from hundreds of years of Buddhist tradition. Finally, non-Asian Westerners *still* project a kind of Shangri-la, Orientalist glow on Asia, expecting that it will be more pure, real, and sincere than what we have in the West.

A visit to Asia can be surprising to those young Buddhists who only knew the dharma through the West. For one, young people expect Buddhism to appear as ancient as it does in stories they read, only to find that Buddhism in contemporary Asia is changing rapidly. The popular squeaky doll of a monk chatting on a cell phone and holding a latte picks up on that unexpected encounter. For two, an up-close view of Buddhism reveals that it is a little less pure and simple than what one reads about. Korean Son (Zen), for example, is not like the Zen most Americans imagine but is a mix of different Buddhisms as well as Confucianism and shamanism. Knowing that Buddhism in Asia is dynamic, in the past and today, perhaps young Buddhists can begin thinking about engaging in a dialogue—especially over the internet—with young Buddhists overseas to see how they're adapting to the immediate needs of modern society.

why do we keep looking over the fence when Buddhism is in our backyard?

Globalization

I recently attended a Jodo Shinshu Friday evening service, attended by older Japanese people. The monk from Japan, in long black robes leading the service, closed with a *metta* meditation that had the flavor of a yoga technique, though he just called it meditation. I asked him after the meeting if this practice was native to his tradition, and he replied that he actually picked it up through living in New York City. He felt it helped the parishioners focus on the other aspects of the ceremony, such as the bells, chanting, and the dharma talk because they were more focused and relaxed. It was surprising to see a fairly traditional group casually bringing in a distant Buddhist cousin from a non-Mahayana lineage. As Buddhisms in America rub off on each other, it will be interesting to see how these new forms will be reinterpreted in Asia, in a time when Asia itself is opening traditions to other influences.

Some say that as economic and cultural globalization progresses in the twenty-first century, so might we see some form of globalized Buddhism. Perhaps there is some of this globalization in Buddhism already. For example, Dharamsala, a Tibetan refugee community in India, now hosts vipassana courses, yoga classes, and has internet cafes. In Burma and Thailand there are international meditation centers built to adapt to Western needs in a host country so that meditators can focus on awakening rather than their GI tracts. We are, in some ways, visiting a Western-influenced Asia, an Asia very different from the one the older Buddhists visited forty years ago.

While a globalized Buddhism would provide some foundation for dialogue among Buddhists from around the world, there are perhaps some problems to it. Many people travel to Asia to spend time in a world completely removed from their own. However, as cultures begin to look more and more like each other, in what place will we be able to really step outside in order to look inside? The same is true of Buddhism: if Buddhisms become a homogenous mass, then what will provide critique, instigate creative analysis, and generate the energy of disagreement that keeps a religion alive?

Young Buddhists might want to be aware of the effects of modernization, globalization, and Westernization on the cultures of Buddhism. With Buddhisms increasingly brushing up against each other at a higher rate than in the past, young Buddhists should consider the balance of preserving distinctiveness against the forces of homogeneity while allowing ourselves to be stimulated creatively by the opening of tradition.

Ethnic and Convert: Two Buddhisms?

Recent takes on Buddhism in America have been careful to distinguish between "convert" Buddhism and "ethnic" Buddhism, two separately developing communities in America. One is primarily made of white, well-educated people who come to Buddhism later in their adult life. They are seen as tending to focus on meditation. The second is composed of primarily Asians, who are Buddhist by inheritance, and they are seen as being Buddhist by going to the temple, making offerings, and not meditating.

In some sense, this observation of two Buddhisms is not without merit. Asian temples here in America have few if any non-Asian members. There aren't many Asians in convert centers, either. This division stems to some extent from language and culture barriers. However, as the essays in this book reveal, despite these barriers there is a lot in common, and with this younger generation, the distinction between the two is becoming blurred. One, there is now a substantial generation of Asians who have lived most of their lives in America, gone to school with non-Asians, and know English fluently. Young non-Asian Buddhists today attend colleges and live in dormitories with a high proportion of Asians in a way that the older generation did not. Second, there is now a small but substantial group of non-Asians

I asked him after the meeting if this practice was native to his tradition, and he replied that he actually picked it up through living in New York City.

who have also "inherited" Buddhism as kids. Likewise, there are some Asian Americans who have converted to Buddhism.

In my view, there is a tremendous amount to be gained if young Buddhists can continue to cross the divide between so-called convert and ethnic Buddhisms. Young Asian Buddhists have said that Buddhism in Asia has gotten too heavy with tradition and isn't evolving to the immediate needs of modern people rapidly enough. Similarly, it seems that Buddhism is losing its appeal to many young Asians in the West, many of whom like to attend Christian church with their friends. Non-Asian Buddhists say that they feel like the Buddhism in America doesn't have enough tradition or institution to sustain families, social needs, and communities in the long term. Some aren't happy with just meditation in meditation centers; they also want chanting, monks, child care and education, potlucks, community outreach, and so on. If the two sides begin to take steps to visit with one another, then there may be a refreshing exchange of ideas and support that may not be generated if the communities continue to develop separately. Perhaps, for example, these religious friendships between the two communities will stimulate more funding of art, music, and dharma events.

Tradition and Renewal

Every generation seeks to translate tradition into something more relevant and useful to the times. In an age where generations are becoming increasingly distinct in our rapidly changing and technologically advancing society, that kind of translation can lead to almost entirely new forms of lifestyle. With every translation, there arises a tension between honoring tradition and creating anew. Do we chant in Sanskrit, Tibetan, and Japanese or go with English? Do we survive on *dana* or charge fees? Do we keep the Buddha statue or just burn some incense? Do we tell misogynist history, rewrite it, or hide it? But to know what is necessary to keep from tradition, what will work from a new creation, and what can simply be refitted is difficult considering that this generation is still looking for answers.

We will need to ask of ourselves how we want to hold the diverse traditional expressions of Buddhism while also keeping Buddhism relevant and fresh to our contemporary experience. Already, there is a range of adaptations: some groups have stripped Buddhism down to a technique or philosophy while other groups are re-creating their perceptions of Buddhist societies in ancient Asia. Even within communities this tension is felt. For example, at a small meditation community a wonderful story is passed around the staff dining hall. One of the dharma teachers bowed before and after his talk to the people on retreat. He received two messages on the bulletin board. One said, "I was deeply offended by your bowing. I did not come here to be converted to Buddhism but to sit and only sit." The other note said, "I was deeply touched by your bowing: it showed a great reverence for the Buddha and his teachings." Thus, even a simple bow highlights the range of how people think of the tradition and renewal of Buddhism.

we will need to ask of ourselves how we want to hold the diverse traditional expressions of Buddhism while also keeping Buddhism relevant and fresh to our contemporary experience.

We are also challenged to think about structures of establishment in Buddhism in the West. Many older Buddhists say that they became part of the counter-culture because they wanted an alternative to the established way of doing things. Now the Buddhist centers that have survived until today have become establishments themselves over the past forty years, with their own pattern and culture of doing things. The question becomes How will these seeds of establishments grow? Will there be more places for Buddhist marriages, youth initiations, funerals, summer camps, primary and secondary education over time? Would it be possible to establish more Buddhist libraries, fund public Buddhist art, initiate stronger community outreach programs from local temples and centers? We can perhaps balance tradition and renewal, establishment and change, if the older generation keeps some flexibility and innovation while the younger tempers their movement forward by honoring the past.

Looking Forward:
A Buddhist Generation Coming of Age

When I set out to discover my generation a few years ago, I didn't expect to meet amazing young Buddhists. Because I hadn't met any young Buddhists, I had a preconception that I would find kids as superficial as the Zen clothing ads in magazines, who wanted to look Buddhist just because it was cool. Instead, I was astounded by the seriousness and thoughtfulness with which my Buddhist peers were unfolding their path in the dharma. They have opened my eyes to ways of expressing the dharma that I had not imagined. Even thinking about teaching meditation to jailed teenagers makes my knees buckle: yet there are young Buddhists who not only do that, but forgo the security of real employment in favor of small grants here and there that require hours of research and proposal to win. Some of these young Buddhists I now see as my teachers. The many young Buddhists I know with remarkable vision and clarity, compassion and wisdom, and thoughtfulness about the world and the environment are sources of inspiration and optimism for the future of Buddhism.

As a generation that has grown up with the foundations of Buddhism laid by the previous one, we are characterized by our greater acceptance in mainstream America. That Buddhism has currency in the broader society may allow young Buddhists to affect dharma in a larger way than seen in previous decades. We might be distinguished from those before us by our greater activity in socially engaged Buddhism and use of the dharma in professional capacities. We may be characterized by our increased interaction between the "ethnic" and "convert" communities, blurring those distinctions. Those of us who were raised Buddhist, acting as a bridge of generations, can perhaps help prevent the same mistakes of the past generation while retaining clarity of vision for the future. How we will handle the issues of teachers, monasticism, lay involvement, religious pluralism, and dialogue with our Buddhist peers in Asia and around the world may unfold in an empowering way. We are challenged, however, by the powerful draw of materialism and the media, by the potentially ungrounding effects of freedom to choose in the spiritual supermarket, and by our own youth and inexperience. We are further asked to think carefully about the effects of globalization, creation of institutions, not isolating ourselves

we are challenged by the powerful draw of materialism and by our own youth and inexperience.

from the previous generation, and balancing tradition with creating anew. This emerging, young generation offers tremendous potential for the unfolding of Buddhism in America.

arhat: (Sanskrit) a fully enlightened Buddhist saint who will not be reborn again into the realm of suffering.

bodhichitta: (Sanskrit) the aspiration to achieve enlightenment for the benefit of all sentient beings.

bodhisattva: (Sanskrit) one who aspires to buddhahood for oneself and all beings.

circumambulating: (English) walking clockwise around a sacred site, thereby creating good karma or merit.

daimoku: (Japanese) literally "title," that is, the title of the Lotus Sutra, *Nam-myoho-renge-kyo.*

dana: (Sanskrit) generosity or the act of giving.

dukkha: (Sanskrit) suffering; the unsatisfactory quality that marks existence.

geshe: (Tibetan) title generally conferred in the Tibetan Geluk tradition on those who have successfully completed many years of monastic education and have thus attained a high degree of doctrinal learning; roughly equivalent to the Western Doctor of Divinity.

gohonzon: (Japanese) The mandala that serves as the object of devotion in Nichiren Buddhism and is the embodiment of the law of *Nam-myoho-renge-kyo.*

gongyo: (Japanese) The daily practice of reciting portions of the Lotus Sutra and chanting *Nam-myoho-renge-kyo* before the Gohonzon in Nichiren Buddhism.

han: (Japanese) wooden board used in Zen monasteries that is struck as a call to meditation.

Hinayana: (Sanskrit) pejorative term meaning "lesser vehicle" coined by the later Mahayana "greater vehicle" school to refer to the early forms of Buddhism, primarily in southeast Asia, often emphasizing individual liberation and the Buddha's rules for monks and nuns. The preferred term for this school is "Theravada."

keisaku: (Japanese) the "awakening stick" used in some Zen schools as a means to relieve muscle tension and dispel sleepiness.

kensho: (Japanese) expression in Zen for seeing one's own true nature, or the experience of awakening.

koan: (Japanese) a teaching tool of the Rinzai Zen school used to stimulate insight, often seeming to take the form of a riddle or paradoxical proposition that cannot be solved by rational thinking.

Mahayana: (Sanskrit) the "great vehicle" of Buddhism that emphasizes the bodhisattva path and salvation of all beings.

mala: (Sanskrit) a string of beads, often 108 in number, used to count repetitions of the recitation of mantras, certain chants, and the name of Buddha.

mandala: (Sanskrit) artistic representation of the Buddhist cosmos in two or three dimensions that can be used in meditation and visualization.

mantra: (Sanskrit) syllables, often Sanskrit, recited to invoke aspects of buddhas, induce purification or insight, grant protection, and so forth.

metta: (Pali) loving-kindness: the sincere wish for beings to be happy and safe.

mudra: (Sanskrit) natural postures of the hands signifying aspects of Buddhist teachings or marks of specific buddhas that can also be used in certain meditation practices.

Nam-myoho-renge-kyo: The mantra of Nichiren Buddhism (which is the title of the Lotus Sutra in Japanese) that is identified as the ultimate reality or fundamental law of life.

Nembutsu: (Japanese) recitation of the Buddha's name, especially by reciting "Namu Amida Butsu" ("homage to Buddha Amitabha") for rebirth in his Pure Land.

pranayama: (Sanskrit) yogic exercises that control and regulate the breathing.

puja: (Sanskrit) ceremonial offerings of food, flowers, incense, water, etc., in recitation, ritual, and meditation.

root guru: one's primary teacher in the Tibetan tradition.

roshi: (Japanese) title for a senior Zen master.

Sakyapa: (Tibetan) a practitioner in the Sakya tradition, one of the four major schools of Tibetan Buddhism.

sangha: (Sanskrit) traditionally refers to the community of Buddhist monastics, but can refer to any community of Buddhist practitioners.

satori: (Japanese) Zen term for enlightenment; sometimes synonymous with *kensho*.

shramanerika: (Sanskrit) a novice nun who has not yet received full ordination but observes the ten precepts (*shramanera* is a novice monk).

shunyata: (Japanese) the principle of nothingness; the inherent emptiness of all things.

stupa: (Sanskrit) sacred monument, often containing relics, that acts as a reminder of the awakened state, serves as a focus of pilgrimage, and is venerated through circumambulation, worship, and prostration.

teisho: (Japanese) a formal dharma talk by a Zen master.

Theravada: (Pali) a school of Buddhism, known as the "Way of the Elders"; widespread in Southeast Asia; in America, closely related to the vipassana and insight meditation schools.

thukpa: (Tibetan) traditional Tibetan noodle soup.

toban: (Japanese) assigned duties such as cooking and cleaning that, at a camp or an outing, are rotated among work groups.

Triple Gem: the three jewels of Buddhism consisting of the Buddha, Dharma, and Sangha.

udumbara: (Sanskrit) a flower that is said to bloom only when the Buddha is living.

upaya: (Sanskrit) "skill in means or method" in guiding beings toward enlightenment, or the ability to effectively expound the Buddhist teachings.

Vinaya: (Pali) the monastic code that regulates the conduct and community of monks and nuns.

vipassana: (Pali) insight into the true nature of existence. Also denotes a form of meditation.

zafu: (Japanese) round cushion used for sitting meditation.

zazen: (Japanese) sitting meditation; literally, "sitting Zen."

CONTRIBUTORS

 Elijah Ary, 28, a native of Canada, was recognized at the age of eight by the Dalai Lama as a tulku, or reincarnation of a Tibetan Buddhist scholar. After spending six years as a teenager in a Tibetan Buddhist monastery in India, he returned to the West and is now in a Doctoral program, studying Tibetan language and religion.

 Seth Castleman, 27, is a teacher, storyteller, and writer. A practicing Jew and a student of Theravadan dharma, he writes about the people, practices, and myths of the Jewish and Buddhist traditions. When not in retreat, Seth teaches dharma to youth and adults incarcerated in America's prisons. He first developed and then directed the Family, Teen, and Children's Programs at Spirit Rock Meditation Center 1994–98, and presently co-directs the Lineage Project in New York City. Seth has trained in Asia and the U.S. under the guidance of U Pandita Sayadaw, Tsoknyi Rinpoche, Jack Kornfield, Christopher Titmuss, Sharon Salzberg, and Joseph Goldstein. He is currently working on a book and film on the life of the Buddha. Photo by Kate Beal.

Amy Darling, 27, works supporting the bereaved family and friends of patients who have died on hospice service through Providence Hospice of Seattle. Her study, work, and travels in Nepal (August '94–December '94 and July '97–Dec '98) were instrumental in redirecting her focus from political science and environmental studies to issues around death and dying. In addition to her work in hospice, Amy is involved in a project of the Tahoma One Drop Zen Monastery (and affiliated sangha) to develop retreats around issues of isolation and burnout for those working in the care-giving professions. Amy practices with both the One Drop group (primarily students of Shodo Harada Roshi) and with the One Pine Hall sangha, primarily students studying and practicing in the tradition of Shunryu Suzuki Roshi. Photo by Courtney Olds.

Jonathan Drummey, 30, grew up somewhere among the ocean, woods, and mountains of Maine. He presently makes his home in Cambridge, Massachusetts with a pile of books to read and a bear bigger than he is. As he wraps up his sabbatical, Jonathan has begun work in a nonprofit to support grassroots patronage of the creative life. Photo by Rachel Mello.

V. Sharif Fennell, 27, was born and raised in the inner city of Boston, Massachusetts. He is a graduate of the University of Massachusetts, Amherst, and attended graduate school at Brandeis University. He has been practicing Nichiren Buddhism since the age of two, with the Soka Gakkai International. Currently, Sharif is applying to medical school.

 Ben Galland, 29, was born in the Rocky Mountains of Colorado but grew up on the beaches in northern California. With a B.A. from Prescott College in Outdoor Education, Ben has spent the last ten years working with kids and adults teaching rock climbing, white-water kayaking, mountaineering, and basic backcountry environmental awareness. He has traveled the world in search of truth and understanding and has come to the conclusion that the wilderness is his place of serenity. More recently, Ben has launched a new career in extreme sports videography and is pursuing his passion to play music.

 Hanuman Goleman, 24, graduated from Antioch College, where he created a senior thesis performance that explored the power of mental constructs in our everyday life. He now works, lives, and plays in Oakland, California.

 Soren Gordhamer, 32, is the author of *Meetings with Mentors* and the meditation book for teens, *Just Say OM!* (Adams Media, 2001). He is co-founder of the Lineage Project (www.lineageproject.org), which teaches meditation and yoga to incarcerated teens. He has practiced Buddhist meditation for sixteen years and teaches meditation at juvenile facilities in the Bronx, Brooklyn, and Harlem. He is currently writing a book about his work with incarcerated youth.

Diane Biray Gregorio, 29, is a Ph.D. student in Sociology and Organizational Behavior at Harvard University. She is inspired by Thai Forest Tradition of Theravada Buddhism, especially the lineage of Ajahn Chah and Ajahn Sumedho, and the Tibetan Buddhist teachings of His Holiness the Dalai Lama. She lives with her partner, Robin, in Somerville, Massachusetts.

Lillian Guild, 31, is writing under a different name.

Claudia Heiman, 29, was born and raised in the Boston area and has lived in Chile, Canada, England, and Yellowstone National Park. A writer and producer of short films and videos, including *Love Bites*, a documentary about fans of British singer/songwriter Morrissey, she currently administers grant programs for individual artists at the Massachusetts Cultural Council. She has practiced the Buddhism of Nichiren Daishonin with the Soka Gakkai International for nearly seven years.

Julia Hengst, 23, is a staff member of *Mandala* magazine, the bimonthly newsmagazine of the Foundation for the Preservation of the Mahayana Tradition (FPMT). She is also publisher and editor of *Mind Trip* magazine, a new magazine for young people interested in good hearts and good minds.

Hwansoo Kim (Il-mee Sunim), 29, a native of South Korea, has been a Korean Son monk since the age of sixteen. An assistant to the abbot at Bulkwang Temple in Tappan, New York, supporting the Korean Buddhist community in the area, he is also a student of Buddhism and Comparative Religion in a Master's Degree program.

Josh Krieger, 30, was born and raised near the bucolic stripmalls of suburban Long Island. After attending college in Boston, he stayed in the area and began to practice at the Cambridge Buddhist Association. In recent years, to support his ravenous Zen habit, he has worked part-time as a computer consultant writing software to help people with disabilities access the internet (www.zafu.com). He is currently training to be a Buddhist hospital chaplain and lives in an ecologically oriented cohousing community in Massachusetts.

Jae-ho Lee (left), 26, attended Hong Kong International School from kindergarten through high school. He graduated from Hofstra University in Long Island with a Business Management Degree. After working for several companies in the New York area, he took a year to begin research on starting a home health care agency and went on to found X-Treme Care in New York City, where he now lives.

Kenneth Lee, 23, is writing under a different name.

 Noah Levine, 29, is the former Director of the Spirit Rock Meditation Center Teen and Family Program in Woodacre, California. He founded the nonprofit organization MBA Project (Mind Body Awareness), which brings mindfulness classes to incarcerated teens. He currently lives in San Francisco, where he is attending the California Institute of Integral Studies, teaching meditation, and working on his book *The Dharma Punx* (dharmapunx.com).

 Jessica Morey, 21, a student of environmental engineering at Dartmouth College, plans to pursue a career as a sustainable community designer or work for an nongovernmental organization in a developing country. She also thinks about becoming a Buddhist nun, to walk a path of a contemplative who is in the service of creating hope and happiness in others through social action. Photo by Matthew Daniell.

 Paul W. Morris, 28, is a graduate of Hampshire College and the former managing editor of *Tricycle: The Buddhist Review*. He has written for magazines and on-line journals, and his published work includes the introduction to the most recent translation of Hermann Hesse's *Siddhartha* (Shambhala Publications) and *One Sound* (Ellipsis Arts), the CD-book accompanying a compilation of Buddhist music. Currently, he is a freelance writer as well as a contributing editor to the website Killing the Buddha (killingthebuddha. com). He lives in Manhattan. Photo by Reeve Chace.

Joshua M. Schrei, 30, is a writer and political activist living in Brooklyn, New York. He spent the first eleven years of his life at the Rochester Zen Center and studied Tibetan Buddhism throughout his adolescence. He is a regular contributor to *Shambhala Sun* magazine, and his essays on Buddhism in America have appeared in *Tricycle, Turning Wheel, Grand Royal*, and *Inquiring Mind*. He recently contributed a chapter to *Zen Teaching, Zen Practice: Philip Kapleau and the Three Pillars of Zen*, published by Weatherhill Press.

Sister Kristine (Thich Nu Pho-Chau), 25, graduated from University of Hawaii–Manoa in Biology. She has trained with the Vietnamese Buddhist Youth Association to be a troop leader in working with children and young adults. Sister Kristine has joined the monastic life and is now on the third year of the Buddhist Training Program at Hayward Buddhist Center, California. Recently she ordained as a *shramanerika* in the Mahayana tradition.

Sister Kristine wishes to express her gratitude to her teacher, Venerable Thich Tu-Luc for giving her permission to write this reflection. She also thanks Venerable Thich Nu Gioi-Chau for finding this opportunity to contribute a small piece to the book.

Adrienne Stauffer, 20, is a senior at the University of Chicago studying Chemistry and South Asian Languages and Civilizations. An active member of Students for a Free Tibet, Adrienne is currently a sector contact, coordinating for over fifty chapters in seven Midwest states.

Reverend Hojo Tone, 31, is a graduate student at Boston University and an ordained Jodo Shinshu minister of the Honpa Honganji Mission of Hawaii.

Cameron Warner, 25, is currently studying Buddhism at the Harvard Divinity School with a focus on the Tibetan and Sanskrit languages. A graduate of Swarthmore College with majors in Religion and Biology, Cameron hopes to continue his scholarly work on the doctoral level. He is a practitioner of the Sakya lineage and a student of His Holiness Sakya Trizin.

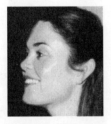

Meggan Watterson, 25, graduated from Smith College with a B.A. in Religious Studies. She worked for two years in San Francisco as a counselor at a residential treatment center for emotionally disturbed children and with a program at an infant center for drug-addicted and abandoned teenage mothers. She is now a Master's Degree student in Comparative Religion, focusing on the divine images of the feminine around the world.

Diana Winston, 33, is the founder of the Buddhist Alliance for Social Engagement (BASE) Program, America's first socially engaged Buddhist training program. She has practiced insight meditation since 1989 with Joseph Goldstein, Sayadaw U Pandita, and others, and spent a year of monastic practice as a Buddhist nun in Burma in 1998. She is a writer, activist, and teacher of meditation, especially to youth, and has taught teens in America and

India since 1993. She also teaches nationally on socially engaged Buddhism. Currently she serves as Associate Director of the Buddhist Peace Fellowship in Berkeley, California. Photo by Alan Senauke.

 Liane C. Yasumoto, 33, earned her B.A. in Social Welfare from U.C. Berkeley in 1992 and is pursuing a career in acting in film, theater, and radio. Liane is one of four wheelchair users represented by one of San Francisco's most reputable talent agencies, "Stars." Currently, Liane is the executive director of the Corporation on Disabilities and Telecommunication (CDT), a Berkeley-based nonprofit organization that works to change the stereotypical images of people with disabilities in the media. From 1997–1999, Liane produced and hosted an award-winning television variety talk show, "In the Groove," for KTOP-TV, Oakland's government channel. She has been teaching various grades at the Berkeley Buddhist Temple's Dharma School for the past twelve years. Photo by Norbert Brein-Kozaewycz.

 David Zuniga, 30, is studying Buddhism and Christianity in divinity school. A Tibetan Buddhist practitioner, he is training as a hospital/ hospice chaplain. David is also an experienced long-distance runner and martial artist who views his athletic pursuits as a vehicle for Buddhist practice.

ABOUT THE EDITOR

 SUMI LOUNDON was born in 1975 into a small Zen community in rural New Hampshire and lived there for eight years with her three sibs and parents. She has a B.A. in Fine Arts from Williams College. A Buddhist, she now lives in Cambridge, Massachusetts, where she is studying Buddhism and Sanskrit as a graduate student at the Harvard Divinity School. Photo by Elsa Wilkens.

Contact Information

To contact any of the contributors or the editor, please send an email to bluejeanbuddha@hotmail.com or write to Name, c/o Wisdom Publications, 199 Elm Street, Somerville MA 02144 USA.

WISDOM PUBLICATIONS publishes authentic Buddhist works for the benefit for all. Our titles include translations of the sutras and tantras, commentaries and teachings of past and contemporary Buddhist masters, and original works by the world's leading Buddhist scholars. Buddhism is a living philosophy and it is our commitment to preserve and transmit important works from all its major traditions.

To learn more about Wisdom, or to browse books on-line, visit www.wisdompubs.org.

If you'd like to receive our mail-order catalog, please write to:

Wisdom Publications

199 Elm Street

Somerville, Massachusetts 02144 USA

Telephone: (617) 776-7416 • Fax: (617) 776-7841

Email: info@wisdompubs.org • www.wisdompubs.org

The Wisdom Trust

As a not-for-profit publisher, Wisdom Publications is dedicated to the publication of fine Dharma books for the benefit of all sentient beings and dependent upon the kindness and generosity of sponsors in order to do so. If you would like to make a donation to Wisdom, please do so through our Somerville office. If you would like to sponsor the publication of a book, please write or email us for more information.

Thank you.

Wisdom Publications is a nonprofit, charitable 501(c)(3) organization affiliated with the Foundation for the Preservation of the Mahayana Tradition (FPMT).